PRACTICALLY DIVORCED

A Woman's
Practical Guide
to a
Successful
Divorce

Jillian Bannister

Practically Divorced
Copyright © 2021 by Jillian Bannister

Jillian Bannister
Jbannister@mydivorceguide.com
www.mydivorceguide.com

All rights reserved. No part of this publication may be reproduced, distributed, or transmitted in any form or by any means, including photocopying, recording, or other electronic or mechanical methods, without the prior written permission of the author, except in the case of brief quotations embodied in critical reviews and certain other non-commercial uses permitted by copyright law.

tellwell

Tellwell Talent
www.tellwell.ca

ISBN
978-0-2288-3020-7 (Hardcover)
978-0-2288-3019-1 (Paperback)
978-0-2288-3021-4 (eBook)

TABLE OF CONTENTS

Blindsided: My story v
Introduction: How to use this book................................... vii
Day one: Overcoming overwhelming................................. 1
The next step: Going public... 9
Strength and support: Building your "A-team" 14
Bench strength: Finding and choosing a lawyer 21
Your options: Understanding the family court system.....31
The process: What happens, when? 41
Your finances: Becoming your own CFO 57
Support: Agreeing on it and getting it 71
Custody, access, & parenting: Finding the right solution.................81
Life after the divorce: Breaking from the past..................94
Conclusion: Your life ahead of you 99
Glossary...101
About the author 107

BLINDSIDED: MY STORY

I'VE BEEN THERE. I was blindsided by a partner who left me when I least expected it. Just weeks after our baby was born, I found out he was leaving me for someone else.

Everyone has their own uniquely painful divorce story. Maybe you've been left for another woman (or for a man). Or you have decided that you have finally had enough of an unhealthy or abusive relationship. Perhaps you and your partner have come to the realization that your marriage has run its course and you both want out. Your personal challenge is unique, but the situation you find yourself in today — negotiating a divorce — is, sadly, not that uncommon.

That's where this book comes in. When my marriage ended suddenly, I found myself without resources, without legal knowledge, and without a clue of what I was supposed to do next. I had to navigate a complicated judicial system, sort out my finances, establish my rights, grieve the loss of my marriage, keep my sanity, get back to work, generate income, and care for my baby. All at the same time. All on my own.

I swore to myself that when my divorce was final, I would use my hard-won knowledge and collect advice from fellow divorce survivors to help other Canadian women in similar situations. I kept track of every mistake I made and every stumbling block I overcame. I made a note of every complicated step I took through the family court system, what I did right, and what I could have done better. I collected a group of women that wanted to share their stories and built a series of surveys to capture their experiences. I gathered everything I learned with the hope that I might one day be able to help other women going through the same thing as me.

This book includes comments from a wide range of women (including me) who have survived divorce and built new lives. All the quotes are anonymous to protect the contributors' privacy. They are all verbatim, describing real events that happened to them and what they learned from them. I hope they help you as much as they helped me.

I wouldn't have made it through the last four incredibly challenging years without the love and support of my parents, the joy of my daughter, my new husband and stepson, and the incredible generosity of my circle of friends, some of whom contributed their own stories for this book.

And I wouldn't have been able to write this book without a team of editors who helped me organize my research and shape my story, who read and re-read my drafts, and who helped polish up the final product to get it to a publishable state. Special thanks go to Richard, Matt, Judy, and Nancy.

Divorce is painful enough. You are going to need to figure out a plan and gather your resources to get through this.

This book can help you.

Jillian

INTRODUCTION: HOW TO USE THIS BOOK

This is a practical guide that will help you from the first to the last steps of your divorce, but it certainly does not have to be read in a linear fashion from beginning to end.

The first chapter is important for everyone whether you're young or old, have been married for one year or twenty, whether you have kids or you don't.

After that, you can continue on page by page or review the Table of Contents and dive in wherever it makes sense to you. You will find tons of useful, relevant information in these pages, but don't feel like you're required to read every single one.

Unless you're a family lawyer, you'll be introduced to a lot of new legal and procedural vocabulary through your divorce. A lot of those words are explained in this book's glossary of terms. Read whichever definitions are most relevant to your situation.

Read, re-read, highlight, make notes, and share. This book is yours. Use it to help you get to where you need to be.

1 DAY ONE: OVERCOMING OVERWHELMING

GETTING STARTED

> *"I could not believe this was happening to me. When I let myself think about everything I was going through and all the unknowns, I felt completely overwhelmed, unable to think clearly — and very sad. Once I started breaking things down into chunks and dealing with things one at a time, I began to feel like I was accomplishing things and making progress."*

First things first. You need to break it down. Here are six things you can start doing today:

1. **Start a divorce journal.** Hard fact: this process may drag on for a couple of years — or more! (The average length of divorce in Canada is about two years.) Start a fact-based journal (not an emotional one — you can start another journal for that), and log any and all events and conversations relating to your divorce: interactions with your ex, dates and length of visits with the children, things you want to discuss with your lawyer. Date everything. For example, Canadian law states a couple can divorce after one year of separation. Clearly define your separation date to avoid complications down the road.

2. **Get professional help.** You will need a lawyer (self-representation has its pitfalls), a financial advisor (this is important), and maybe a therapist. Keep an open mind about seeing a therapist, even if it's something you've never done before. This may be the most stressful experience of your life, and you will need to be in the right state of mind to proceed effectively. Your doctor, your lawyer, and/or your friends can refer you to a therapist. Chapters 3 and 7 have advice on dealing with a financial advisor, and Chapter 4 can help you find a good lawyer.

ABUSE

If you are being abused in any way, don't be intimidated or afraid to call the police or a women's shelter for advice — and always inform your lawyer.

---

3. **Close any joint bank accounts.** If you have joint bank or investment accounts, call your bank and find out if you and your ex are able to withdraw money independently of one another, or if your accounts require a co-signer. If you have co-signed any credit cards, lines of credit, or other forms of debt (besides your mortgage), contact your bank and discuss your options. If you can't cancel your joint credit card, ask about lowering your credit limit. If you don't have a credit card in your name, get one.

"My ex used our joint card and racked up huge expenses. I was the primary card holder, so I was left holding the bag."

4. **Protect your privacy.** Change the passwords on your voicemail and email accounts, bank cards, and social media sites. Unfriend your ex online.

5. **Ensure the privacy of your email.** You need a safe, private, and isolated place to store emails about your divorce proceedings. Create a new account with a brand new password or create a

separate folder or inbox in your existing email account (if you feel your existing email is safe from your ex). Within your email account, create sub-folders (e.g., legal, property, finances, scheduling, etc.) for all the different kinds of emails you exchange with your ex, your lawyer, and any professional and personal resources you are consulting. Important: keep ALL emails from your ex no matter how insignificant. You never know when they will be helpful to your case.

6. **Get your paperwork organized.** Collect, copy, or photograph any financial/property documents in your home (much of this can be found online). Don't hand over anything, sign anything, or agree to anything without consulting a financial or legal professional. You should also print important emails and file them in a binder or file folder by date (or at least throw them all in a box so you know where they are). It may seem like a waste of paper, but if, for some reason, you can't access your email account, you will still need this information.

"After our separation, my husband came over and urgently asked me to sign some financial documents. I was feeling vulnerable and didn't want to fight over every little thing, so I signed them without consulting anyone. Big mistake. The resulting financial mess haunted me throughout the entire divorce process. It took me ten years to recover from it."

Seriously. Do these things today.

DEFINE YOUR GOALS

> *"At the outset I did some serious soul searching and wrote down my main objectives around support, custody, and visitation. My lawyer was impressed when I brought him a copy — and it helped me stay focused on the important issues."*

You will gain a measure of clarity and control by writing down realistic goals for what you want to achieve at the end of this process. Think about what you want financially, where you want to live, what you want for your children, and how you will define their relationship with you and your ex.

Keep your goals at the beginning of your fact-based journal so you can remind yourself of what's important. Referring to your goals will help you stay focused on the important things and keep you from getting stalled in difficult negotiations. Use this checklist to help you define your goals:

Family/Parenting
- Define your vision for your children's relationship with your ex (if they are young) or how you will support your children's relationship with your ex (if they are older).
- Define your children's relationship with you.
- Define how you will settle major parenting decisions, such as choosing what school your children will go to.
- Determine how you will settle minor parenting decisions, such as what sports your children will participate in.
- Decide what kind of relationship you want with your in-laws.

Finances
- Define spousal support and child support needs.
- Sort out debt payments.
- Think about whether you will sell your house.
- Consider saving for your children's education.
- Think about how you will manage your retirement savings.

Legal
- Ask yourself what you expect from your lawyer.
- Determine what kind of lawyer you want: someone aggressive or someone focused on mediation.

Health/Lifestyle
- Consider how you will maintain your mental health.
- Make time to take care of yourself physically.
- Make time to be with your children.
- Think about what you want your relationship with your ex to look like in the future. You will be involved with your ex for many years to come (whether you want to or not).

TOP FIVE MISCONCEPTIONS ABOUT DIVORCE

It will be quick. The average divorce takes about two years, but some take longer. Much longer.

It won't be very expensive. Divorce is not cheap. The average divorce costs between $25,000 and $50,000. Some highly conflicted divorces can run well over $100,000.

My ex will be reasonable. Divorce can bring out the worst in some people. Your ex is looking out for his new interests. So should you.

My lawyer will handle it. Your lawyer is there to help and advise you, but it's actually your job to be clear, advocate for yourself, and track every detail.

My ex is to blame for all this, so he won't get anything in court. Not true. Since 1986, Canada's Divorce Act permits divorce after one year's separation with no requirement to prove "fault" by either spouse, and most lawyers recommend filing a no-fault divorce

> application. It may not feel fair, but a person's marital conduct (unless he has committed a crime) will not affect his entitlement or rights.

DEFINE YOURSELF

> *"Any time I felt I was losing control or going to a 'bad' place mentally, I reminded myself of the kind of person I wanted to be throughout the process. I chose to be constructive — and it paid off. I earned the respect of my lawyer and everyone else around me. And I believe that translated into them working harder for me or providing extra help along the way."*

What kind of divorce would you rather have: constructive or destructive? A constructive divorce is healthy. A destructive divorce is unhealthy, and no matter how justified your destructive behaviour might seem at the time, it just ends up hurting everyone involved.

Ask yourself who you want to be, and write that description in your personal (emotional) journal where you can read it whenever you wish. Extreme hurt, anger, and sadness can make it hard to stay on the high road, and you may need to remind yourself of your goals on more than one occasion. Write down key words or phrases as touchstones to help bring you back to where you believe you should be.

> **TO DO**
>
> Get your journal. Take some time to define how you want to behave and be perceived throughout this process. Do you want to be tough but fair? Stand up for yourself more than you have in the past? Be more knowledgeable and organized? These phrases can become your mantra for when times get tough or emotions run high.

No matter how justifiably angry you are or how difficult your negotiations may become, reminding yourself that you are consciously choosing a constructive approach to your divorce will save you a mountain of grief and sadness.

Each time you feel you are treading close to destructive territory, remember this: how you "are" will impact your mental state and how others interact with you, including your friends, your lawyer(s), and your ex.

Remember, being constructive doesn't mean giving in. In fact, you are probably more likely to get what you need if you remind yourself of the three Rs of constructive negotiation:

- **Rational thought**
- **Realistic plans**
- **Responsible behaviour**

Write these down and repeat as needed.

Be persistent in pursuit of what you need and maintaining your personal balance. If you make a mistake and lose your cool, remember to forgive yourself, try to refocus on your goals, and move on.

TOP FIVE MAJOR CHALLENGES ABOUT DIVORCE

The money. Figuring out the finances — past, present, and future — is long, involved, and the opposite of fun.

Keeping your cool. If you have children, they will be relying on you more than ever. Maintaining family stability and well-being in the midst of upheaval will be difficult.

Juggling. You will have to maintain your existing schedule of work and childcare while making time for lawyer's appointments and court dates.

> **The courts.** They can only do so much. You won't be able to count on the legal system to ensure that agreements and orders are being fulfilled. They can issue orders, but they can't enforce them.
>
> **A steep learning curve.** Unless you are a divorce attorney, you probably know next to nothing about family law. Get ready for a crash course. See Chapter 5 to learn more about the Family Court System.

Going through a divorce takes a lot of energy and feels like a long haul. However, take a breath and internalize this fact: the process of divorce does not last forever. This book will help you through it.

2 THE NEXT STEP: GOING PUBLIC

SHARING THE DETAILS IN PERSON

> *"Communicating the end of the marriage to others is delicate. When you are distressed about the separation, it's hard not to talk about your ex in a bad light, but the costs can be high. Forcing friends to choose between the two of you can be painful — best not to put them in that situation. I tried to tell the whole ugly story to as few good friends as possible, which meant that the vast majority of our social group wasn't exposed to all of it. This seemed to make the transition easier. But it's also important to realize that you can't be responsible for people's reactions to the news: sometimes they will overreact because of their own fears of divorce. There isn't much you can do about that."*

Telling your social and professional circle that you and your partner have split is hard, but it has to happen eventually. Protect yourself emotionally by waiting until you have some sense of yourself, where you stand, and how you are going to be.

Share only what you have to. Stick to the basics. Ask yourself: will it help this person, or help this person help me, to know more? More often than not, the answer will be "No."

Be selective in who you tell at first. Having one or two trusted outlets to talk things through is important and will make it easier for you to maintain a calm, rational state of mind at key moments. Once you know you have a few discreet resources you can rely on, you can start telling other people. On a practical level, you will have to tell your child's daycare or school, your neighbours, your boss/trustworthy co-workers, and your babysitter/caregiver.

Get your story straight and keep emotion out of it as much as you can. As tempting as it may be to discuss some of the details of your separation — especially if you are aggrieved or angry — revisiting the painful play-by-play over and over again with everyone you speak to is not healthy for you.

Getting people on your side by sharing the nitty-gritty details feels good at the time, but most people I spoke with agree that indulging in a steady stream of negativity wears you out. We each have a limited amount of energy. It's better to save your energy for you and your children. Remember, your plan is to focus on the constructive. Talking too much to the wrong people can actually be destructive.

From a legal standpoint, you should always be careful what you say about your ex, yourself, and your situation. Your comments may come back to bite you if you share details with an untrustworthy connection.

> *"Just be very careful talking about your personal life with friends, whether on Facebook or in person. You never know who will pass on the info. And always be careful talking in public, especially in a small community. You never know who is listening."*

HOW TO FACE FACEBOOK (AND OTHER SOCIAL MEDIA)

> *"I think social media with one's ex should be avoided altogether, unless the divorce is truly amicable. My ex abused Facebook from start to finish: he broke into and spied on my account; and then the first thing he did once he was served papers was to launch a Facebook campaign against me, in which all our Facebook friends were forced to choose sides or unfriend us both."*

> *"Friends had warned me against even discussing the divorce on Facebook (either on my page or in personal messaging), as one of them got into trouble with a judge over comments she made about her ex on Facebook during their divorce process. Social media should be used for far lighter subject matter. As with anything else you commit to writing, you should never post anything on Facebook that could be used against you in court in any way."*

Social media and managing an online presence adds a whole new layer of complexity to the divorce process. Communicating in the era of social media means there are a few extra things to keep in mind as you work your way through the divorce.

- **Unfriend your ex and his family members** while you are working out the details of the divorce. You can reconnect with people you want to stay in touch with after you settle, but while you are still negotiating, you need to be careful about who knows your news.

- **Don't email your separation news.** If you aren't close enough to meet with or call this person then your message can wait. Avoid using social media to convey anything about your divorce, even the relationship status section.

- **Avoid using your online accounts as a place to vent or post**, even if you think you are anonymous.

- **Don't torture yourself by checking your ex's Facebook status** or looking for pictures of your ex with someone new.

- **Change all your passwords.**

> *"Keep your personal life out of Facebook. The more negative talk you put out about your ex, the worse you look. Don't gossip, don't speak ill, try to leave your emotions off Facebook or other social network sites as much as you can ... I unfriended my ex immediately. I have many friends who are still his friend on Facebook and tell me about*

> *what he is posting — as if I want to know!!! I just ignore their comments."*

THE BEAUTY OF EMAIL

> *"At the beginning of our separation, my ex would call me and verbally abuse me. After the first few times, I thought, What am I doing? and started to let all unknown calls go to voicemail. I saved abusive messages, played them for my lawyer, and he decided if they needed to be transcribed or not. Now I communicate via email only."*

Modern technology isn't all bad. While social media has a few traps you should avoid during a divorce process, email is one tool you can use to your advantage.

Start following this rule of thumb regarding communication as early as possible: communication with your ex will take place primarily through email. Organize your inbox to separate your divorce-related emails, and be consistent in using this as your only form of communication with your ex until you can verbally communicate constructively. Email will also be your primary form of communication with your lawyer.

Sticking to email offers many advantages. Email lets you take your time to compose objective, fair, and non-emotional messages that you can save and review before sending. If you have difficulty with face-to-face confrontation or have trouble making requests, email takes the pressure off and lets you plan out how to properly convey your thoughts. An "email first" policy will also save you from dealing with an emotional phone call when you least expect it or aren't feeling up to it. You can note that your ex has emailed you and respond within a reasonable time frame but only when you feel ready and without disrupting your day with unnecessary drama.

If you do find yourself communicating over the phone, take a minute after you finish talking to type up notes on the conversation if you discussed anything important — and save it. Send an email as soon as possible asking him to confirm the details for your records.

Unlike a phone conversation, an email is a detailed, documented record of an exchange that can be used in court. An ex who doesn't answer emails or sends threats and abusive remarks will leave a paper trail. Although you may be tempted to share any nasty comments or unflattering rants on Facebook (you're only human), just don't.

Save everything and share it with your lawyer.

Compose your messages carefully, stay calm and in control, take a breath before sending, and you will have nothing to regret. Respond only when necessary. Ignore inflammatory remarks. Don't make statements you aren't prepared to follow through on. Always stick to your point.

Finally, communicating with your ex doesn't have to be confrontational. If you stay cool, you can keep the lines of communication running smoothly, which is better for everyone in the long run. Send the occasional positive email about your children's accomplishments or a thank you for the swift arrival of a document. This will help break up all the negative stuff you and your ex must continually wade through.

> *"At keys moments of the year, my ex and I communicate daily, but most of the time we try to keep it to once a week, on Sundays. It is better for both of us to know that there won't always be a time bomb email waiting for the other in their mailbox."*

Starting to speak publicly about your separation or divorce is a huge milestone — and it's not easy. Once it's out there it's real and your life will change. One of the most important things to remember is that you don't have to do it alone. Read on to learn how to build an "A-team" of friends, family, and professionals who will be your support and guide you through this challenging period.

3 STRENGTH AND SUPPORT: BUILDING YOUR "A-TEAM"

PERSONAL RESOURCES

> *"My mother was phenomenal. She took me in, and I had the opportunity to live with her part-time for five months during the transition to divorce. She listened, she cooked, she listened some more, and was always there for me. I feel very fortunate that she was there, and I feel closer to her as a result of the divorce."*

After reading Chapters 1 and 2 you are starting to get some things organized. And you've decided how you are going to act and how you are going to communicate. You've started to share your news, and now you are dealing with a load of reactions, comments, curiosity, judgement, and support.

This is where you find out who your friends are and whom you want to have on your team.

You aren't going to get through this alone, and you need to gather the right support team around you before you move forward.

The superheroes you need:

The empathizer. Everyone needs one of these. She/he might be a sibling, long-distance friend, or a neighbour you didn't know was so awesome. Whatever form they take, an empathizer is always a great listener and has probably had some experience with the emotional rollercoaster that is divorce. *Judgement level: 0*

> "My most important personal resource was my friend who had been through divorce herself; she had helpful suggestions and just listened. This friend constantly encouraged me to pursue a fair deal. I called it tough love, done gently."

The pragmatic pal. This person's superpowers kick in when you just need to get stuff done. Maybe they aren't as comfortable with the emotional side of things, but they are smart, supportive, and organized. If you need a kick-starter to help you move past the emotional and into the practical, the pragmatic pal is the one you need. *Effectiveness level: 10*

The persistence coach. There will be times throughout this process when you run out of steam and need someone to help get you back on your feet. Like any great coach, your persistence coach will pump you up when you're down and get you focused on fighting for yourself and for your goals. *Self-pity level: 0*

> "I found I got tired and, when that happened, it was easy to let something slide that shouldn't have. I needed a friend who could reinvigorate me and get me back into fighting mode."

The expert. There is someone in your circle who is (or knows someone who is) a lawyer, financial advisor, or psychologist. Use them as a sounding board to validate other advice you are receiving or to help you find the contacts you need to build your key resources team. *Smarts level: 10*

The socializer. There is some serious value in that upbeat friend who's out and about all the time. She/he may not be able to listen as well as your empathizer, but she/he will get you out to a movie, art exhibit, drinks, or dinner. You need this; it can't be about the divorce all the time. *Fun level: 10*

People are kind, and they want to help. Accept help from friends who don't fit into any of your superhero categories but still want to pitch in with cooking, babysitting, carpooling, and grocery shopping. You have your hands full, and you need to stay positive. **Let people help you.**

VILLAINS TO AVOID

Some people show their strength in a crisis, others, their weakness. As soon as you get a whiff of any of the following from anyone in your family or among your friends, avoid them as much as possible.

> *"My mom was incredibly unhelpful. She was raised with very old-fashioned notions of what constitutes a 'successful' marriage. She couldn't understand why I might want to leave a relationship when the other party 'had a great job' and 'didn't hit or abuse me.' I realize now, after years of reflection, that she had great intentions and certainly didn't want to see me suffer (financially). However, her initial feedback was beyond terrible."*

The moralist. People who feel it is their duty to tell you that divorce is morally wrong and the root of all evil in society today. They're not the life of the party.

> *"Don't talk to anybody who is judgmental, carrying their own baggage, negative, or gossipy."*

The gossip. This is the frenemy who shows an avid interest in the details of your divorce so she/he can broadcast them far and wide. Your pain is not someone else's entertainment. Cross this person off your list.

> *"Friends often respond with lots of support, but sometimes their own fear of divorce can get in the way ... I quickly realized that people's responses often had more to do with their own lives than with my situation."*

The projector. It may be your divorce, but others may use your situation as an excuse to take stock of their own relationships/situations, with you as their sounding board. You don't have time for this right now.

> *"My dad was furious with my ex. He even talked about getting him knee-capped! I know he wasn't serious, but I didn't need to manage his emotions and mine."*

The uber-empathizer. Some friends and/or family members may get even more worked up than you are about the daily ups and downs of the divorce process. Dealing with their anger as well as your own is simply not productive.

> *"I was pretty stunned at how my ex's family and colleagues took sides right away ... I found it pretty shocking how many people just took his word for things and cut me off."*

Your ex's friends and family. People you once knew well might become strangers overnight when they feel they're forced to take sides. It's best to avoid them as much as possible until things become clearer.

On the flip side, if your separation is more amicable, this group doesn't have to be in your bad books. It's OK for you and your ex to give them permission not to take sides. After all, maintaining these extended relationships may be valuable to you in the short- and long-term.

PROFESSIONAL RESOURCES

> *"The child psychologist gave me concrete understanding of my son's needs and based this on facts and studies. This allowed me to feel confident that what I was fighting for truly was in the best interest of our son."*

Now that you have your personal superheroes around you and the villains kept at a safe distance, it's time to bring in the professionals. Some professionals you already have, and others will be entirely new to you.

Lawyer. A divorce is an important legal proceeding, and the first professional resource you will need is a good lawyer. Important criteria: your lawyer should have a reputable family law practice, be priced within your range (hourly rates can range from $300 to $750), and be conveniently located (you may be required to attend a lot of meetings). Set up initial meetings with more than one lawyer (three should be ample) so you can make a thorough assessment before you decide on who will represent you.

SELF-REPRESENTATION

More than half of litigants come to court without a lawyer.[1] Why do people do it? Primarily, it's the money. But the unfortunate fact is that judges prefer individuals who work with lawyers because that is the way our justice system is designed. "Dealing with 'self-reps' imposes heavy burdens on judges, court officials, and opposing counsel. This leads to frustration and contributes to a second barrier, delay."[2]

"I didn't have enough money to pay for a lawyer, but in the end I wish I would have figured out a way to make it work. Self-representing was stressful — and I lost some pretty key things in the end."

Therapist. Apart from your lawyer, a therapist (or a similar professional) will be one of your most important resources. You need someone to listen to you unconditionally about the emotional aspect of your situation and help you maintain the balance you will need to move forward. This may be covered by insurance (hopefully you can find a therapist that is). Even if this is an added cost (therapists' fees range from $60 to upwards of $200 per hour), it will likely be worth it.

"I felt vulnerable only at the beginning. Once I took care of myself, my needs and my mental health, everything fell into place. I needed to reflect on and process the underlying issues that led

---

[1] Alex Ballingall, "Justice Denied: Huge Legal Bills Push Many to Self-Represent in Court," *Toronto Star*, April 11, 2016.
[2] "Access to Justice: A Societal Imperative," Remarks of the Right Honourable Richard Wagner, P.C. Chief Justice of Canada, October 4, 2018.

> to the breakdown of my marriage. It was necessary for me to do that with the support of a professional versus a family member or friend. I needed to ensure a level of honesty, transparency and confidentiality with that experience, so my preference was a professional therapist."

Parenting co-ordinator or social worker. Many lawyers will recommend using a parenting co-ordinator — a licensed social worker or psychologist who will help you deal with child custody, visitation scheduling, and childcare decision-making. These individuals specialize in conflict resolution between parents with the objective of establishing a parenting plan (see Chapter 9 on child custody and access for more details on parenting plans). Costs vary, and you and your ex will need to enter into a mediation agreement to implement the parent co-ordinator's recommendations.

> "My ex and I saw a parenting co-ordinator at the beginning. My ex was a bully and a very difficult person to reason with. Our parenting co-ordinator helped me establish boundaries and gave me the language to have a productive conversation with my ex about our kids."

Financial advisor. No matter how good you are with money, you are likely very stressed by your finances at this time. Studies show that people experience a serious financial decline in the first few years after separation/divorce. You are no longer sharing financial responsibilities with your ex, and you'll need to have a strong grasp on all the moving parts of your finances — from income to expenses to life insurance and pensions. The best thing you can do to alleviate this stress is to find a financial advisor.

These are some (maybe all) of the key resources you need to manage during and after your divorce. It may seem like a lot, but you'll definitely need each of them to one degree or another over the next few years. They say it takes a village to raise a child. The same could be said about divorce.

> *"All the resources served to work together. I would accept something in therapy and apply it in mediation. I would do something practical with my financial planner and deal with the fear it brought up in therapy. And so on."*

OTHER PROFESSIONAL RESOURCES YOU MAY NEED TO ACCESS

Real estate agent. Your divorce will likely result in a change in your living situation — whether you sell, buy, or rent. It's important that you find an agent you trust who understands your needs and timelines.

A private investigator. Yes, you really might need one. Get the contact information for a PI and keep it on hand, just in case. **The law is all about making sense of information, so the more information you have, the better.** If you are dealing with an unreliable ex, you may need help with tracking down car license plates or work scenarios, or providing documentation of alcoholism, drug use, or unhealthy living conditions in order to protect your children.

Doctor. Your general practitioner and your children's pediatrician are important resources for both physical and mental health. Tell your doctor and your children's doctor what your family is going through so they can keep a close eye on you for stress, depression, alcohol consumption, and overall well-being. Your doctor can recommend a therapist for you and a child psychologist to help your child understand what's going on.

All of the contributors to this book shared the notion that divorce shows everyone's true colours. Not just yours and your ex's — but your friends and family too. Realizing who your true friends and supporters are is a massive fringe benefit of divorce (even though it may not feel like it right now).

4 BENCH STRENGTH: FINDING AND CHOOSING A LAWYER

MAKING THE CALL TO MAKE THE CALL

> *"It's a long, emotional process, so you need to be comfortable with the person, be able to work with them, and be sure they aren't just a "yes" person. I have a great relationship with my lawyer, as I feel he looked out for my needs and was strong for me when I wouldn't have been. I needed him to protect me, as you can be very vulnerable when discussing the practical elements of separating assets. You need someone who is familiar with the longer-term repercussions."*

Making that first call to a lawyer is a big step. You're acknowledging to a stranger that you want out of your marriage, and that professional resource has the power to help you do just that.

You are going to spend a considerable amount of time with your lawyer. You need to choose a strong and experienced advocate with whom you are comfortable sharing information, who works effectively with you to understand your perspective and situation, and who has a philosophy and approach that fits for you and your goals. Some lawyers specialize in court work, others in settlement outside of the courts.

You will also need to do some soul-searching and think about what kind of lawyer you want to work with. Here are some questions to consider:

- Is preserving your relationship with your ex important to you?
- Can you and your ex work "in good faith" together, even under the current situation?
- How well do you stand up under pressure? Can you handle conflict well? What support do you need to make smart choices?

COMMON MISCONCEPTION:

Once you have made an initial call to a lawyer and booked a meeting, the lawyer cannot take a meeting with your ex. The truth is, this is a grey area; technically you need to have a meeting, so focus on using this process to find the right lawyer for you, not to "outsmart your ex."

Your best option is to find a family lawyer through a referral from a friend or another lawyer. Although you can do research online (search "family law" and the name of your city or town), the best lawyers stress that finding one through a referral is the superior approach.

> "A client told me that her previous lawyer asked them to write a review online after they had met once. How can you write an informed review after meeting someone for one hour? This is the risk with using the web as your main way to find a lawyer."
>
> - Advice from a notable Canadian family lawyer

Most of us have few, if any, dealings with lawyers outside of real estate or business transactions. Once you have gathered a list of potential family lawyers, prepare to make the phone call to set up a consultation.

Depending on the size of the law firm, when you call the lawyer's office, you may be speaking to the receptionist or directly with the lawyer. To prepare for this first conversation, get out a pad and pen and write out a simple script to prompt you through the call:

"Hi – I am in the initial stages of a separation and looking for a lawyer..."

"I have been referred to you/your firm by..."

Be prepared with information that includes:

- How many years you were married.
- The basic reason for separation (keep it short).
- How many children you have.
- Your employment status.
- Your current living arrangements.

Take notes to help you with your assessment after you've finished talking to each potential lawyer. And don't be intimidated in this consultation: you're the client, and the lawyer is the service provider. You're the one holding the cards here.

Don't forget to ask about:

Fees. Find out if there is a fee for the initial consultation (there usually is). Ask about their retainer fee and the hourly rates for litigators, junior lawyers, and other staff.

Style and approach. Ask the lawyer about her/his style or approach. For example, how many of their cases go to trial vs. mediation or collaborative practice? Does he or she consider interests and values or a strictly legal analysis? Does he or she work with other divorce professionals, and if so, how?

Structure. Who will be your day-to-day contact: the lawyer or a junior associate? If it's the latter, you should meet that person as well to ensure they are also a good fit.

Us vs. them. If your ex already has a lawyer, ask your prospective lawyer about your ex's lawyer's approach, whether they can work effectively together, or how they plan on addressing this. Divorce law is a narrow field, and your lawyer may know the opposing lawyer.

Availability. Many lawyers are booked, but don't be deterred. Ask if they have any other lawyers they can recommend.

Experience. Find out how many years the lawyer has been practising in your city/town and what approach they have focused on. Working in the field of separation and divorce is all about philosophy and experience.

COSTS EXPLAINED

Retainer is an amount paid up front. When you choose a lawyer, you will be asked to sign a retainer form and to send it in with a cheque. Most retainers are between $5,000 and $15,000, and will be put toward your future legal bills.

Disbursements are out-of-pocket costs taken on by a law firm on behalf of a client for court fees, photocopies, expert testimony, etc. These costs are on top of the lawyer's hourly legal work.

Legal consultations may cost approximately $500 per meeting. In many cases, the firm will credit you for the cost of the initial consultation if you proceed with the firm as your representative.

THE CONSULTATION

> "I walked into my lawyer's office with a vision of what I wanted and my priority issues... They were realistic goals, and although it was expensive and time-consuming to pursue them, I did achieve them. We stayed laser-focused, and that worked in our favour."

Now that you've tracked down at least one lawyer and made an appointment, you should bring the following to your consultation:

- Your journal — a succinct, nuts-and-bolts version of your story. Lawyers find it valuable if you write according to the chronology of events. Use dates and bullet points, keep the language simple, and include pertinent details only.
- Your marriage certificate and the deed to your house.
- A list of your income, assets, debts, and financial circumstances.
- A list of your objectives.
- A trusted friend or family member for moral support and to help with note taking.
- A list of questions.

Plan to be forthcoming with all details and actively involved in the process. Remember to leave the emotional aspects of the separation to your therapist or personal support team.

MAKING YOUR CHOICE

> *"Chemistry is important. I wanted to feel like my lawyer was 'on my side' and not just taking on my case. I needed to feel that he was my advocate."*

You've had your consultations and gathered all the concrete information you can about each candidate. Now think about what kind of people you work well with. Do you like a softer touch or are you good with someone who is curt but practical? Are you detail-oriented or strategic? Think about some of your personality traits that might affect your decision regarding choosing a lawyer.

It's also important to think about your ex's personality, then and now. Does he rise to fight or become intimidated? Will an ultra-aggressive lawyer increase your ex's aggression or diminish it? You don't want to be intimidated by your ex, but you also don't want to create a constantly explosive dynamic.

> "As soon as my ex was on the other side of the negotiating table, the gloves came off. He was unpredictable, volatile, and mean. My advice is to stay focused on you and your goals, not what he is saying or emailing. Don't let him take you off course."

Personality and style will be important for you to consider, not only when you are looking for a lawyer, but also when you are considering what procedural path (mediation or collaborative practice vs. the courts) you want to take. You need to feel comfortable with your lawyer and confident in her or his ability to get the job done. Sometimes it's a matter of following your gut.

> "My negotiation style was weak when I first started this process. I was very uncomfortable with conflict, so I knew I needed a tough lawyer who would advocate on my behalf."

It's important you understand that lawyers are there to help you. And they will help you, especially if you find one with whom you communicate and work well.

Remember, your lawyer *is*
- Your advocate
- Working for you

Your lawyer *isn't*
- Your therapist
- Your friend
- Your administrative assistant

WORKING SUCCESSFULLY WITH YOUR LAWYER

> "Be honest. Don't put your lawyer in a position where they don't have all the facts. You need to be very open with your lawyer about your financial situation, your assets, and your goals for your children."

Lawyers work best when they have ALL the facts — and you will get results if you stay "on point" with your goals. Use these best practices to develop a positive working relationship with your lawyer.

Be clear about your goals. At this point, you may feel you have fine-tuned your goals. Expect they will change as your case progresses, and be sure to continually reference them with your lawyer.

Be honest and upfront. You may think a certain detail is not relevant, or you may feel uncomfortable revealing some information about your marriage. This will only weaken your case and your relationship with your lawyer. Don't be shy: they have heard it all.

> "I was nervous and embarrassed bringing up my ex's abusive behaviour — it felt like a reflection on me. I was glad I did as it helped my lawyer truly understand the dynamic of our marriage and, with that knowledge, he was more aggressive with my ex in court."

Be prepared to work. Remember, you know your case better than anyone else. Especially if you are going to court, be prepared to spend a large chunk of time researching, reviewing, and providing feedback on your affidavits and other documents.

> "Before each court date, be prepared to have ample time to think about and review the affidavits your lawyer has put together. Ask your lawyer about the timing of when you can expect the first draft so you can plan to review and provide feedback shortly after. Also — get familiar with Track Changes in Word. It helps the process!"

Stick to the plan. You and your lawyer are setting your course now. Don't let anything your ex says or does take you off strategy. Lawyers don't work well with clients who don't stick to the plan.

Do-it-yourself. This is as much for you and your bank account as it is for your relationship with your lawyer. The less admin your lawyer is doing, the more she/he can do the job for which she/he was trained. Take care of as much administration as you can: photocopying, transcription of voicemails, and putting together timelines.

> *"Ask your lawyer for similar cases and read them for ideas on other information you can provide or things to consider."*

IT'S OKAY TO SAY "GOODBYE" TO YOUR LAWYER

Once you have gone through your first court submission (likely for a case conference), you will have a good sense as to how the relationship with your lawyer is working. If you aren't sure, ask yourself these questions:

- Did we work well collaboratively?
- Did she/he listen to me and take my objectives seriously?
- Do I feel like my lawyer is my advocate?
- Is my lawyer helping me take a realistic and reasonable approach?
- Do I like my lawyer's team?
- Do I feel like my lawyer and her/his team had time for my case?

If you answered yes to these questions, you are in a good place. **If not, you may want to consider switching lawyers.**

> *"Keep a running list of the questions you have for your lawyer. Peppering your lawyer with questions via email is disorganized and costly. Also, keep a written list of your objectives handy and make sure your lawyer understands and is onside with your objectives. Always refer back to your objectives to make sure they are addressed in any court documentation."*

If you are doing everything you can to help your case and you are still not happy with your lawyer's performance/approach/style, you need to switch lawyers.

> *"My biggest strategic mistake was not leaving my first lawyer soon enough. I stayed with him because change seemed ominous, and I thought it was better to stay with the 'devil you know.'"*

It makes sense. You are dealing with so much change in your life, and you just want something stable. Destabilizing your life with another major shift feels scary and intimidating, especially when you are dealing with such a complex subject. You might be wondering:

Who am I to say my lawyer isn't good enough? I've invested so much time, effort, and money. Is switching lawyers at this stage a bad idea?

Don't doubt your instincts. If your lawyer is no longer a good fit or if, for whatever reason, you are no longer on the same page, you aren't communicating, or you don't feel supported, find a new lawyer.

- **Step 1:** Go back and speak with the previous lawyers you met with or spoke to — or canvass all your new "divorce" peers about their lawyers. You will have a much better sense of what you are looking for this time around.

- **Step 2:** Make sure your new lawyer can take you on. You will likely have to pay another retainer or sign a fee commitment document. Note: any unused retainer fees from your previous lawyer will be refunded to you.

- **Step 3:** Let your current counsel know you are terminating the relationship by voicemail and email. If you have been working with a junior lawyer, it's nice to let him/her know too.

- **Step 4:** You will need to sign a Change in Representation Form, which your new lawyer will provide.

- **Step 5:** Give your existing lawyer a week to get the files to your new lawyer. Give your new lawyer a list of important dates coming up, any undocumented idiosyncrasies of your situation, and your list of objectives.

Finding the right lawyer may take a few tries — and that's OK. It's imperative that you feel listened to, respected, and supported by your lawyer. On the flip side, hiring a lawyer doesn't mean you leave all the work to them. You will have to "dig-in" by finding and providing documents, thinking through and owning your decisions, as well as not letting your emotions take the lead. The best lawyers like working with clients that roll-up their sleeves, get engaged in the process, and work with the facts. Once you have struck that balance, you will feel positive momentum with your case.

5 YOUR OPTIONS: UNDERSTANDING THE FAMILY COURT SYSTEM

A BIRD'S EYE VIEW

> *"I originally thought: my husband cheated on me and was extremely emotionally and verbally abusive, so I have a strong case. Of course we are going to trial! But as it turned out, with the help of our lawyers, we were able to mediate our way through it. It wasn't easy — it was still very painful — but I was able to move forward with my life more quickly and didn't waste an unbelievable amount of time and money."*

The family court system is complicated. There is no such thing as a linear path to success. Couples might start out trying mediation, move to arbitration, and, if that doesn't work, go back to mediation. The intention of the court system is to get couples to try every possible path before going to trial before a judge. Why is that?

- It's much less expensive.
- It puts the couple in control of decision-making vs. the risk of a judge making decisions for you based on standard options.
- It's typically much faster.

- It's less adversarial and, even though it may not seem like it at times, more mentally healthy (especially if kids are involved).

What are the options? Outlined below is a list of possible approaches ordered from least to most contentious. Understanding these will help you make more informed decisions and work more efficiently with your lawyer.

Uncontested divorce. The least adversarial scenario is an uncontested divorce. This situation happens when both parties mutually agree to end the marriage and often see themselves better as friends. In this scenario, both partners agree to the reasons and terms of the divorce (including financial aspects and, if there are kids, the parenting arrangement). These divorces need only one application that is reviewed and approved by the court to make sure it meets the requirements of the law and is fair. Even for an uncontested divorce, it is a good idea to have a lawyer help draft and review the application before submitting it to the court.

Mediation. Mediation is a process where a couple works with a neutral mediator to resolve the terms of the separation. With mediation, there is no obligation to hire a lawyer, but sometimes one or both of the parties will work with a lawyer to review terms of their agreement or even sit with them at the mediation table.

> *"We chose mediation, and it worked well for us. It was quite fast (we had an agreement within three months of the separation), and it enabled/encouraged me and my ex to co-operate rather than see ourselves as combatants. The disadvantage of mediation is that it can drag on if one party is not particularly interested in settling quickly. If one party wishes/needs to settle quickly, he/she is at a disadvantage since delay/obstruction by the other party is difficult to manage aggressively."*

The practice of mediation is a relatively new field and different from other approaches because a mediator has no power to rule on an issue. It was developed to be less formal and provide a high degree of flexibility by enabling couples to set their own agenda and come up with creative solutions to their issues.

As a result, couples that choose mediation retain control of their decision-making and typically experience less conflict. However, it takes a very conciliatory, open-minded couple to resolve all of their issues through mediation.

Mediation only works when both parties:

- Have some level of goodwill and a willingness to consider the interests of the other (versus solely focusing on their own interests).
- Trust each other (at a moderate level).
- Understand the key issues.
- Feel comfortable advocating for themselves (on their own if they are not represented by a lawyer, and to some degree if they are using a lawyer in conjunction with a mediator).

Mediation is also a tool used by the courts to resolve the "easier" issues even while a couple is "in court" if it's believed that a particular issue can be worked out without a judge's ruling.

Your lawyer will typically suggest some names of mediators and work with your ex's lawyer to settle on a mutually acceptable mediator. But it's important to do your own research too! Check out the websites of the recommended mediators, talk to any friends about mediators they have used, and, if possible, have any initial phone calls with the suggested mediators. Like researching your lawyer, it's important that you understand their style and approach to understand if it's a good fit for your personality and situation.

Once you have agreed upon a mediator, you will meet with them and:

- Complete an intake document requesting a chronology of events and your objectives/interests.

- Agree to the rules of engagement regarding the mediation process.
- Work collaboratively to develop an agenda that will determine the issues you will tackle first.

In a typical mediation process, you and your ex will meet separately with the mediator. The mediator will take notes and isolate the key issues for discussion. You will reconvene as a group with the mediator facilitating the negotiation process between the two of you. The mediator will draft any decisions made, and it is wise to get your lawyer to review these decisions before you approve them.

There is another aspect of mediation that is important to consider. There are two types of mediation: closed and open. In the former, the whole process is kept private (that is, not admissible in court). Many couples use this to maintain privacy if they feel they can achieve an agreement outside of the courts. With open mediation, your information can be used later in court if necessary. "Open" mediators are generally more expensive, but they can be worthwhile if think you might end up back in the court system.

Before you embark on mediation, talk to your lawyer about the implications of "closed" or "open" mediation sessions on your case.

COLLABORATIVE DIVORCE

> *"We opted not to enter the court system, and I'm glad we made that decision. The financial burden of the divorce process was hard enough. The expense of it all actually encouraged us to pursue mediation and collaboration versus litigation or the court system. We just wanted to divide our assets, develop a co-parenting plan, and move on."*

Like mediation, collaborative law is a new area of practice that is also designed to be flexible, reduce conflict, and empower the couple. The main difference between collaborative law and mediation is that the parties are represented by collaborative lawyers and sign a "no-court" participation agreement. The lawyers are charged with advocating for their clients, while simultaneously working as a team to facilitate a settlement. If a settlement is not achieved and the couple decides to go to court, they must hire a separate litigation lawyer. This is done to remove the threat of court from the equation, which motivates the participants to focus on finding solutions to their issues (rather than how to attack and win at the expense of the other).

For this approach to work, it requires both parties to:

- Believe that both parties are on an equal playing field.
- Practise honesty and full disclosure.
- Be motivated to be directly involved with the crafting of the settlement.
- Have the ability to see the interests of others rather than focus on protecting their own.

Another benefit of collaborative law is that collaborative lawyers often have relationships with other family professionals that can help establish new structures and help deal with the emotional and financial issues of divorce. Some examples include:

- Social workers with expertise on children who can speak to you, your ex, and your kids about what is happening.
- Co-parenting experts who can help work out parenting plans and deal with the emotional issues of divorce.
- Financial planners who provide support on budgeting, financial planning, and tax strategies.

ARBITRATION

Arbitration is often used when a couple can't resolve issues through mediation or collaborative law. It is more formal and close to a court experience, but you are essentially hiring a private judge (who is typically a senior lawyer) to resolve your issues.

The most important difference with arbitration is that **the arbitrator (not you) makes the final decision**. In fact, you are legally bound to obey the arbitrator's decision *even if you don't agree with it.*

Arbitrators can make decisions on custody, access, support, and other financial issues. However, they can only make decisions that they are asked to resolve. And they cannot grant a divorce — you will still need to submit an application to the courts for that.

Because arbitration is like a less formal court case, you are required to prove that you had legal advice before proceeding, but it's also beneficial to have a lawyer to help you understand what relevant evidence you need and to craft your argument.

At the hearing, you and your ex will present your arguments and outline what you think is a fair solution. Witnesses can also be called. After each of you has presented, the arbitrator will make a decision, and you are bound to abide by it.

HEADING TO COURT

> *"Avoid court as much as you can. Preparing for hearings takes a lot of work — and it can cost $15,000 just to prepare for one hearing. It pushed my legal bills sky high."*

Everyone says that no one wins when a divorce goes to court. It's true. Even when it appears that one of the spouses somehow got the upper hand in a decision, it doesn't ultimately feel that way. There is just too much loss — emotional, temporal, and financial — in the process of going to court to ever consider someone a winner. Divorce that goes to court takes longer and costs more: the average divorce costs $25,000 – $50,000, but couples with highly contentious situations may spend well over $100,000. It's not unheard of to take out loans and second mortgages to cover the costs.

Family law is adversarial in its very nature, and going to court ramps up this antagonism. It can bring two reasonable people to the brink of rage.

And if your separation is already fraught with issues, going to court will likely make matters worse.

If you think your court experience will look like an episode of *Law & Order*, think again. You'll likely have many days in court, and you won't be making speeches on the stand to a jury of sympathetic individuals.

Before you jump to court, you need to ask yourself, "Have I done everything possible before resorting to this?"

> *"The law is set up to protect both sides. Judges and courts have no interest in the emotional he said/she said. Some things will seem unfair and anger you, but other things will work in your favour — there is good and bad, and nobody wins."*

So why would anyone go to court?

The short answer is that you have no other choice. One or both of you can't take a step back and see the advantages of understanding and respecting the other person's perspective in order to work it out.

On the other hand, it's also vital that you are realistic and honest about who and what you are dealing with (even if it's not what you want).

KNOW THE PERSON ACROSS THE TABLE

Divorce takes two people, so it's important that you think about whom you are negotiating with — and look at yourself in the mirror. Are both of you motivated to be fair and open to compromise or are you or your ex combative and unwilling to bend? This will impact which approach you end up taking.

If you ultimately think you are heading to court, make sure you find a lawyer who "gets" your situation, understands why the out-of-court options available probably won't work, and who has the experience and skill to do the job you need done (See Chapter 4, "Finding and choosing your lawyer").

YOUR OPTIONS — AN OVERVIEW

Process	Details	Pros	Cons
Uncontested/ Do-It-Yourself (DIY)	Complete the required forms and draft a separation agreement with or without a lawyer (although with a lawyer is recommended).	Cheaper and quicker.	Room for error and potential regret. Don't sign anything until you've had it reviewed by a lawyer.
Mediation	A neutral mediator, often a lawyer or trained social worker, helps you work through the main issues through negotiation, keeps the conversation on track, and (hopefully) gets you to a reasonable separation agreement.	Less adversarial. More control in the hands of the individuals. Cheaper if you are using a mediator without a lawyer.	Increased costs with both mediator and lawyers involved. Nothing formal to keep the parties engaged in the process. "Closed" mediation documents are not usable in court (if you end up there).
Collaborative Law	Individuals and their lawyers make a formal commitment to stay out of the courts and look for a mutually acceptable settlement.	You have a lawyer to support you. Professional team available to help with other issues. Both the law and your interests are considered. Customized outcomes. Maintain control.	A lengthier process. Work is inadmissible if you end up going to court.

Arbitration	Both parties must agree to arbitrate and have proof of legal counsel. A trained neutral third party makes binding decisions. Useful when couples are not successful with mediation but want to stay out of court.	Avoids court. More private and quicker than court.	Final decision is given to someone else. Decisions are based on the law vs. interests. Can be more lengthy and costly than mediation (as you are paying for both lawyer and arbitrator).
Court	Lawyers are hired to draft documents and litigate in their clients' interests.	Confidence of having a lawyer who can advocate for you.	Expensive. Public. Exceptionally time-consuming and lengthy. Very confrontational and often destroys relationships.

Now you have a basic understanding of the system, right? Wrong (sort of). The landscape of family law is always evolving. As separation and divorce rates increase and the courts are more backlogged, courts and family law experts are constantly looking for ways to evolve the system to make it more efficient, productive, and healthy. So, don't be surprised if a new option, step, or term pops up during your journey.

> *"The first time I went through the court process I started with a case conference. A few years later when my ex filed a new application to change our court order, we had to see a Dispute Resolution Officer before we could move to the case conference stage."*

The good news is that you don't have to keep up to date on the changes to the system. Your lawyer will know the required steps and all the changes that have taken place. A good lawyer will walk you through the steps so you know what to expect.

DECISION TIME

After reading this chapter you might want to take a step back and think about what approach is best for you and what is realistic based on your situation. Here are some questions to ask yourself:

- Are you able to hear what you need to hear rather than what you want to hear?
- Are you able to let go of some of the "small stuff"? Can you live with "It's going to have to be good enough"?
- Can you take a long-term perspective and not make decisions based on today? Imagine where you want to be in five years.
- Are you working with people who understand and respect your needs and have the right skill sets?

The process you choose and the professionals you choose to work with are two of the biggest decisions you will have to make. Remember, you are in the driver's seat. This is your life. By educating yourself (which you are doing by reading this book) and engaging in the process, you are going to make better, more informed choices that are right for you.

6 THE PROCESS: WHAT HAPPENS, WHEN?

SPEAKING THE SAME LANGUAGE

> *"The law has its own language. If you don't understand the words and the system, this will put you at a distinct disadvantage. It is so important to be well-informed and understand all the implications of the decisions you make."*

All divorces are different, and there is no way to understand everything involved and every possible outcome. But what you can do is get up to speed on the common procedural steps outlined below and the distinct lawyerly language used when dealing with on the following pages. This will help you work with your lawyer more effectively and possibly give you an advantage over your ex.

LEARNING "LAWYERESE" — TERMS YOU NEED TO KNOW

Affidavit – A written statement voluntarily made under oath that provides facts that could be of consequence in court.

Applicant – The person who files for divorce. This is done using a general application.

Case conference – An initial meeting where all parties come together to discuss the case in front of a judge.

Court order – An official proclamation by a judge. A court order can be as simple as setting a date for trial or as complex as custody arrangements and support payment schedules.

Draft order – An order drafted by your lawyer in advance of the motion hearing. It outlines the terms you are seeking.

Factum – A short document concisely summarizing an argument. A factum may include a list of relevant case law to support the argument.

Financial statement – A sworn document that includes a statement of income, assets and liabilities, and other financial information that might be relevant (i.e., special or extraordinary expenses). See a more detailed description in Chapter 7.

Interim or temporary order – An official proclamation by a judge that is effective only for a limited time or until the final decision of the court. There are also interim/temporary orders issued depending where you are in the process.

Motion – A written or oral application made to a court or judge to obtain a ruling or order directing that some act be done in favour of the motion applicant.

Motion hearing – A legal proceeding in which both sides can present their arguments and provide factual evidence. Motion hearings are typically more limited in scope than trials.

Pre-trial hearing – The occasion when the parties identify the actual issues for trial. Orders and directions may be obtained in a pre-trial so that the trial will proceed more efficiently.

Questioning or examinations for discovery – A pre-trial occasion during which your lawyer can question your ex with your ex's lawyer present, or your ex's lawyer can question you with your lawyer present in an effort to acquire new information and/or to confirm on-record information they already have.

Respondent – The person who responds to the general application.

THE APPLICANT AND THE RESPONDENT

The first thing you and your lawyer will do is either file for divorce as the applicant or respond as the respondent. If you are the applicant and there are issues such as custody, child support, or a parenting schedule to be contested, you will complete a general application. The general application will provide a history of the relationship and the separation to date, and set out what you are asking for regarding support, child custody and access (if applicable), and division of property. If you are the respondent, you will answer to a similar document, stating your position on these same issues.

Once the application has been served (given to the respondent, in person), the respondent has an opportunity to review it and must file an answer and a financial statement (if support or property issues are involved). There is typically a 30- or 60-day deadline to respond depending on where the respondent resides.

> ### LOCATION, LOCATION, LOCATION
>
> In most cases, an application must be issued in the jurisdiction where one of the parties lives. If custody/access is an issue, the application must be issued in the jurisdiction where the children reside.

The application/answer process can be quite stressful because, for the first time, you are reading your ex's demands — and his take on your marriage — in a legal document.

> *"My ex served me his response at my office. I sat down and read it — it was full of lies and unrealistic demands. It all became real right then — I knew I was going to have the fight of my life."*

You will also begin to piece together your financial statement with your lawyer as well as your affidavit to support your case.

> ## WHICH COURT?
>
> In Canada, there are three different courts you can file with:
>
> **Provincial Court of Justice:** These courts can only deal with issues relating to support, custody and access, and paternity and child protection.
>
> **Superior Court of Justice:** In addition to the above-mentioned issues, these courts can deal with divorce, property division, and common law trust/equity claims.
>
> **Family Court of the Superior Court of Justice:** These courts can deal with ALL the family law matters listed above, as well as adoption.
>
> Don't worry, your lawyer will know which court to file with.

If the divorce is uncontested, meaning you can come to a separation agreement on your own, you would file for a joint application. With the help of your lawyer, you would then work through a lot of paperwork between you and your ex's lawyer to complete the process.

DIVORCE VS. SEPARATION AGREEMENT

Divorce is the end point, the legal dissolution of your marriage, the cancelling of your duties and responsibilities to each other.

In Canada, you can get divorced if you meet the three following criteria:

- You've been a resident for at least one year in the province where you plan to file.
- You're married.
- You've been separated for a year.

A separation agreement (or sometimes called a settlement agreement) details how it's all going to work regarding your finances, property, support, and custody. A separation agreement has two main parts:

- **The parenting plan.** How you will organize your parenting responsibilities.
- **The financial agreement.** How your finances and property will be divided.

CLASS IS IN SESSION

In some provinces, you are required to attend an information session in order to file an application or response with the courts. These sessions are designed to explain how the system works, the impact of separation/divorce on children and adults, as well as legal options and resources.

THE END GAME: YOUR AGREEMENT

> *"I had no idea I would spend thousands of dollars as a result of our lack-of-details separation agreement. Make sure your separation agreement covers all bases and leaves no assumptions."*

Your end goal is to have a signed separation/settlement agreement that you feel good about and can live with. It takes time, compromise, and good negotiation skills to get what you want. Here are some things to think about as you go through this process:

Align your separation agreement with your goals. Start by reviewing the goals you previously documented. Through a clearer understanding of the system or the negotiations with your ex, these hopes may no longer be practical, or you may find you are pretty close. In either case, make sure you can live with what's in the agreement — you can't take it back once it's done.

Be as specific as possible. Insist on detailed clarity surrounding all major issues regarding finances, custody, and support.

> *"Make sure your separation agreement stipulates the maximum allowable distance for joint custody. We agreed to fifty kilometers (I never imagined he'd move) and, one year following our separation, he moved 49.2 kms away! Needless to say, that was a significant inconvenience for the children and for me. He later moved back to the city (thank goodness)."*

In other words, be as detailed as you can. If you feel there's something that hasn't been accounted for, propose including it.

> *"If communication is bad now, it will get worse, sometimes for quite a while, if children and co-parenting are involved. If this is your situation, try to get the right kinds of details in your agreement so you don't have to discuss and negotiate every little thing."*

Succeed first. Start with less difficult issues so you have positive momentum going into the more challenging parts. And if you can concede something that's not on your top priority list, it may go a long way in getting you what you want later on. Talk to your lawyer about this strategy.

Understand there are limits. Be as specific as you can without trying to predict the future. As time passes, things change in ways you would have never imagined. If you have an agreement that insists upon revisiting certain issues with honesty and goodwill as tenets, then you have one that will stand the test of time.

Take your time. Rushing simply means you are missing things or trying to avoid things that you shouldn't. While you might be desperate to settle and get this process over with, don't give in on anything in order to settle quickly. You could find yourself with less than your fair share or in an awkward position.

Be prepared for the worst. If each of you has hired a lawyer, then the combativeness inherent in the system has you in its grip. Each of these lawyers is hired to represent your interests, and this is what they will do. You may have had reasonable discussions with your ex before hiring lawyers; don't be surprised if this is no longer the case.

Leave the relationship at the door. Bringing the baggage and the pain to the negotiation table doesn't do anyone any good. When it's the two of you in professional company, be stoic, practical, and smart. It pays in the end.

> *"I did learn that it was pointless to discuss terms when either of us was in an emotional state about the actual separation."*

Think long-term. You might find yourself squabbling at times over something immaterial or a frustrating incident that happened last week. Try to look beyond this.

> *"I called my lawyer to ask his advice when my ex started taking some of the furniture out of the house. His response was, 'Do you really want to fight about furniture? We can, but my advice is to stand your ground and fight about the truly important things.'"*

Be patient. The system is slow and there will be delays on your side and on his.

> *"I know several people for whom the ex's delay caused them to compromise just in order to get a settlement signed."*

Don't rush to judge. There may be offers or ideas you receive from your ex that seem outrageous and/or downright wrong. If you can, don't respond right away. Listen calmly to everything that is being put on the table and think about it.

Pay attention. Listen closely to what he wants, without comment. Don't show whether this is significant to you or not. You can use this as a bargaining chip down the road.

> *"It took a lot for me to realize that negotiation means giving up something. By listening closely to his demands and addressing*

them, I was able to position what I wanted more effectively. It became a good life skill!"

YOUR FIRST LEGAL MEETING

"Looking back, I am so glad I chose an extremely seasoned and well-respected lawyer (even if he cost a lot more). The family law system is extremely complicated, with lots of documents to file and processes to follow. Judges respect processes being followed. I am positive his experience helped move things along faster and gave me an advantage."

After you've filed your application or responded to your ex's, you'll begin preparing for your first legal meeting with your ex, whether it's at the mediation table or at a case conference.

You will eventually have to meet face to face with your ex. You will have approximately four to six official get-togethers, with divorce professionals present, before you come to an agreement. If you end up actually going to trial, you could have as many as ten meetings.

What to expect:

Unless you have decided on an uncontested divorce, it will be more than just the two of you in this legal meeting. Keep your expectations low.

Your first meeting may be disappointing, with nothing much getting resolved. The reason for this lack of progress is that these first meetings are almost always administrative, and the judge or mediator is trying to understand the nature of the case.

"For my first case conference I prepared a statement just in case I was allowed to say anything — not a chance. It was very administrative and only accomplished determining our next court date."

"We went through mediation, and our first meeting was frustrating and seemed to create more barriers to getting the separation sorted out than not."

> *"Besides having to sit and look at him face to face, it went well. We set out the guidelines and signed paperwork to ensure both of us agreed to follow the rules. We did collaborative law."*

> *"We used mediation; it was tough. The mediator first met with each of us for fifteen minutes alone. She told me that women can usually get the children if they walk away from the finances, so I should consider that first and foremost. That didn't seem right to me, so I had to go back to the drawing board."*

> *"If your first meetings in mediation and collaborative divorce are disasters, realistically, it may be a good indication that you will end up going to court."*

NAVIGATING THE COURT SYSTEM

The court system is convoluted, clunky, and slow. Most family court systems are back-logged — and in some cases archaic.

> *"I couldn't believe it but my judge handwrote all of his orders — my lawyers had to interpret his handwriting, type it up, get approval from my ex's lawyers, and then send it back to the judge's administrative assistant to get an office court seal. The process easily took a month."*

The general order of events of a court process looks like this:

- Case/settlement conference
- Motion hearing
- Pre-trial hearing and questioning
- Trial

At any time during the process, you and your ex can opt to go through mediation to resolve an issue, or either party can present a settlement offer on all or any specific issue in order to avoid going to trial. Settlement offers typically come with an expiry date and time, which is usually the day of a court appearance.

With the exception of costs, the details of a settlement offer can't be discussed in court or included in any documentation filed with the courts, such as an affidavit.

CASE/SETTLEMENT CONFERENCE

This is your first official meeting with a judge and your lawyers. In some provinces, it is called the case conference; in others, it's called the settlement conference.

This first meeting is an opportunity for the parties to sit down in a court setting (yes, you will be asked to "please rise" when the judge enters the room) and explore the chances of settling the case.

The case/settlement conference will:

- Identify which issues need to be decided.
- Review other ways to resolve the issues (such as mediation).
- Decide how the case will proceed (e.g., the timing of court hearings, exchanges of documents, etc.).

There may even be a follow-up conference if the judge thinks an agreement of any sort can be ironed out in the short-term.

In many cases, a court order will come out of your case/settlement conference. It could be an interim (or temporary) order for support, custody, parenting plan, additional documentation required, or your next court date so you and your ex have some rules in place while you finalize things.

MOTION HEARING

The next phase in the process is a motion hearing where both parties present their arguments orally and the judge asks questions about the case. A motion can be made at any time after the first case conference.

There is a lot of legwork and anxiety leading up to a motion hearing. The legwork comes from you needing to provide even more details and documentation to help your lawyer further build your case.

> *"I kept a visitation log, a child support log, nasty emails, etc. I also tracked down assets and documents that were in his name ... I felt like a PI!"*

The anxiety comes from the fact that, if you are here, your divorce has become more heated and adversarial. This is also a time where many people realize the real impact of handing off your decision-making to a judge.

> *"I was confident in my case, but unnerved by the fact that someone else was going to be making decisions on my and my daughter's behalf that could impact our lives forever. I didn't have a choice because my ex walked out of mediation — but it was an overwhelming feeling."*

Here is what you can expect:

- **Kramer vs. Kramer.** You will arrive at your motion hearing a few minutes early to meet with your lawyer. Your names (e.g., "Kramer vs. Kramer") and the judge to whom you are assigned will be on a docket list outside the courtroom.
- **It's public.** Be prepared for other people (lawyers and their clients) to be in the courtroom. The judge will start by asking each of the legal representatives to help him/her determine the priority and order of cases to be heard.
- **Last but not least.** If you are bumped to the end, don't worry. Stay alert and pay attention. Watching the judge in action will give you an opportunity to see his/her approach and learn about the process.

> *"My case wasn't date sensitive, so I was at the end of the list, which actually worked out because I got to see how the judge handled each case. It really helped me understand the process and how decisions get made in court."*

- **Prep for shorthand.** You will not get a transcript of the exchange, so try to take detailed notes to help you remember the events of the day.

   "Taking notes is crucial because you will want to remember what happened, and your family and close friends will want to know the details. In my case, there were some funny lines from the judge considering how offside and ill-prepared my ex and his lawyer were, so I wrote them down for some levity."

Again, a court order will most likely be issued after your motion hearing. A good lawyer will have prepared a draft order in advance to give to the judge for the sake of efficiency.

PRE-TRIAL HEARING AND QUESTIONING

A pre-trial hearing is a mandatory procedural step before going to trial. It is intended to ensure that the parties are ready for trial and that there are no unnecessary delays or surprises once the trial starts. It is also an opportunity to try to resolve as many issues as possible to shorten the trial or to eliminate the need for a trial altogether.

Questioning (or examination for discovery) is a request that may come out of a motion or pre-trial hearing. It's quite rare for a divorce case to get to this point, but if a party needs more information or clarity on information (such as financial information) prior to going to trial, an examination for discovery is set up. This typically takes place in a boardroom or office and is like a cross-examination where your lawyer can question your ex (or your ex's lawyer can question you) to acquire or confirm information.

> ## QUESTIONING BEST PRACTICES
>
> **If you don't know** or are unsure of the answer, say, "I don't know." It's honest and better than saying something you might regret later.
>
> **Answer questions efficiently and accurately.** Don't be vague: your ex's lawyer may try to pin you down uncomfortably if you generalize.
>
> **Wait a few seconds before answering** any questions so your lawyer has an opportunity to strike the question if need be.
>
> **Keep detailed notes** and a chronology of events — this will help you provide clear, concise answers.

TRIAL HEARING

This is it — the final step in the court process (unless, of course, you are considering an appeal). The structure of your trial will have been determined through the pre-trial hearing. Some trials allow each party to testify, call witnesses, or be cross-examined. Some are a lot more limited in scope.

Again, a good lawyer will provide a draft order (along with your affidavit and evidence) outlining the terms you are seeking as well as a factum listing relevant case law the judge can refer to when making a decision.

> ## ASK BEFORE, NOT AFTER
>
> Ask your lawyer before your trial date if they are preparing a draft order and factum. If they aren't, you may need to reflect on some of the ideas in Chapter 4.

After the trial hearing, the judge will consider all the evidence and case law and make a decision in the form of a written document (or endorsement). Your lawyer will prepare a written order based on the judge's decision, work with your ex's lawyer to get final approval, and ensure it is signed and sealed by the appropriate court. Each party will receive a copy of the signed order.

TRAPS TO WATCH OUT FOR

Intentional delays

> "The delays in producing financial papers on my ex's part resulted in the divorce taking at least twice as long, if not more, than I was initially led to believe it would take. We still don't have a date for the final hearing."

Delaying is a legal, financial, and personal strategy, and a major source of frustration. Delays can erode people's patience, self-confidence, and mental balance. Your opponent in court may delay producing financial papers, delay making crucial decisions, or delay meetings. Delays result in increased legal costs and a longer divorce process.

> "He delayed his decision on whether he wanted to buy me out of the house and when he would provide me with my money (if he did buy me out). He also delayed in providing the times he would be available to meet for mediation and in sharing his financials (income from new job, value of his inheritance, etc.). It was endless."

Unfortunately, there is not a lot you can do with respect to delays. The only way you can affect this is to abstain from playing the "delay game" yourself. Be patient and ask your lawyer to point out this pattern to the courts, mediator, etc. They will take notice.

> "Once, my ex didn't show up but his lawyer did, so we continued on with the proceedings. Before that date, he had already cancelled twice, so we didn't accept a change to the date. Of course, postponing court dates always prolongs the experience but, more importantly, it increases costs because even if you agree to delay, someone from

> *each legal team has to show up in court and state to the judge they are OK with the postponement!"*

It's a good idea to get your lawyer to send out a communication to remind the other party of the upcoming task decided upon in the case conference or hearing. That way it's clear and things can be tracked.

Orders and non-compliance

The system is only as good as the people in it. The court can issue orders but they aren't necessarily obeyed. You may have to go back to court for enforcement.

> *"My ex was court ordered to supply a complete financial statement over four times … he never did, but kept getting chances. It was very frustrating. From the start, I played by the rules and provided complete and accurate information. He never did — and it didn't seem to catch up with him … until the end."*

The bottom line is that if your ex doesn't want to accept responsibility for a court order, it will probably take you several visits to court to obtain a final order on any issue.

> *"I started with a temporary order for support after my first court date, then went back four times before I got a final order … the judge kept giving my ex chances to do the right thing — he never did."*

See section on support enforcement and MEPs in Chapter 8.

Congratulations! You have completed a crash course on the legal system. By learning about the system, some of its structures and procedures, as well as some common legal terms, you have a leg up on your ex. You will have a clearer picture of what is going on and where you are at in the legal process. You will also be able to relate better with your lawyer and give informative updates to your "A-team." Keep reading on to learn another one of the most important aspects of divorce: your finances.

7 YOUR FINANCES: BECOMING YOUR OWN CFO

THE BOTTOM LINE — YOUR FINANCIAL STATEMENT

> *"Looking back, I wish I had someone who conveyed to me just how expensive it is to rebuild a home with all the necessary essentials: three beds, living room, dining room, etc. I had NO concept of what a financial hit that would be. Also, being a liberated woman, I thought I didn't need to ask my ex for money (spousal or child support). I earn my own living, and I'll figure it out. Again, it would have been great to have someone explain the implications of a split on those terms."*

Your finances and property have most likely become a serious concern since you separated from your ex. It gets complicated when you begin to figure out how possessions will be divided up.

You need to know as much as possible on this subject because many women experience a socio-economic decline in their lifestyle after divorce.

If you have already started building your case with your lawyer, then you've begun completing your financial statement.

> **TIP**
>
> Keep your financial statement up to date — even post-divorce. In most cases, an annual review will take place where you and your ex will be required to share any financial changes that might impact support.

Every Canadian jurisdiction, in some form or another, requires a financial statement and necessary attachments. Unless you are an accountant, completing your financial statement is probably a major point of stress and is the last thing you want to deal with. It is, however, a good place to put all the pertinent facts regarding your finances, and it brings clarity to your financial picture.

The following is a breakdown of what is in a financial statement:

- Income
- Expenses
- Assets
- Debts

> **FROM PAPER TO PIXELS**
>
> It's now time to take your first big organizational leap (if you haven't already) and open up a spreadsheet in a program like Microsoft Excel. It's easier if you use one document with several worksheets for everything.
>
> If you aren't comfortable with spreadsheets, don't be afraid to ask for help from one of the "experts" on your team or see what you can learn doing your own research on the internet. They can either quickly show you how

to create simple addition and subtraction formulas or set the spreadsheet up for you.

This is a small but valuable step. Starting on the right organizational foot early on will:

Reduce overwhelming feelings of stress.
Prepare you for the long-term.
Enhance your working relationship with your lawyer.

INCOME

You need to piece together the last three years of your income, and that most likely means digging into other files (or piles!) in your home.

Here is a list of some common income sources. For the most part, you can look at your previous years' tax returns (T4s and Notices of Assessment) for this information.

- Employment income, including commissions, tips, and bonuses.
- Self-employment income.
- Employment Insurance (EI) benefits.
- Workers' compensation benefits.
- Social assistance income.
- Interest and investment income.
- Pension income including Canada Pension Plan (CPP) and Old Age Security (OAS).
- Child Tax Benefits or Tax Rebates.
- Registered Retirement Savings Plan (RRSP) withdrawals, capital gains, etc.
- Any bonuses or non-cash benefits your employer might cover (e.g., company car or memberships).

It is common when determining income to gross-up non-cash benefits by a certain percentage to calculate a pre-tax value of the benefit. For example, if your company pays you a car allowance, this could impact the stated income in your financial statement.

> *"My ex was claiming a very low employment income, but all of his company cars and memberships were benefits he received from his companies. In our calculations, we grossed these benefits up to reflect a more accurate income amount for him that we could present in court."*

EXPENSES

Calculating your expenses is a little more complicated than calculating your income because it can take time to breakdown your bank statements and find receipts or other supporting documents.

> *"Do it in Excel, make a list, step away from it, and then get past financial bank and credit statements to jog your memory about those expenses that may only happen once or twice a year."*

Start by documenting your current expenses rather than your proposed budget. You need to know your current financial state before you jump into planning mode. Your current expenses spreadsheet will also be a good benchmark for developing your proposed budget.

> *"I just had a big 'to do' list with timelines where necessary (i.e., for setting up utilities, bill payments, insurance, etc.). I also did a rough budget in Excel and kept adding to it as I knew what each of my monthly costs would be. This allowed me to determine the mortgage payment I would be comfortable with."*

> **STEP BY STEP**
>
> **Step 1:** Use the categories provided on your financial statement as a baseline (see list below).
>
> **Step 2:** Start with the easy stuff: your mortgage, car payments, etc.
>
> **Step 3:** Break up the information you don't know into bite-sized pieces, then give yourself a timeline to get that information.

Here's a list of some standard expense categories and items you will want to document:

- Housing (rent or mortgage payments)
- Utilities (electricity, gas, cable, internet)
- Household expenses (food, household supplies)
- Childcare costs (daycare, nanny)
- Activities (programs, classes, camps)
- Transportation (gas, tolls, public transportation costs)
- Health (insurance premiums)
- Personal (clothes, grooming)
- Entertainment (subscriptions, eating out)
- Vacation (trips)
- Investments (including automatic RRSP or Registered Education Savings Plan [RESP] contributions)

ASSETS

Finally, something in the credit column! In family law, your assets are referred to as your matrimonial property. This is property that you and your ex acquired during your marriage, with a few exceptions:

- Gifts
- Inheritances

- Trusts
- Settlements
- Personal injury awards
- Personal effects
- Business assets
- Property exempted under a marriage contract or separation agreement
- Family heirlooms
- Property acquired after separation

> ### INHERITANCE
>
> In most cases and in most provinces, inheritance is exempt from being divided between spouses. It is considered excluded property. This is true if the inheritance in question was kept separate from your other property.
>
> However, if you helped pay for your matrimonial home with some of your inheritance, this money gets locked into this asset, and in almost all cases, the proceeds from the matrimonial home are split 50/50.

Real estate. One of your most important assets is any property you and your ex own. Whether it's your matrimonial home or vacation property, these assets will always be the first point of discussion.

> ### MATRIMONIAL HOME
>
> Every property in which a person has an interest and that is — or, if the spouses have been separated, was at the time of separation — ordinarily occupied by the person and his or her spouse as their family residence.

With respect to other assets, taking pictures and getting copies of any supporting documentation of anything valuable in your home is worth the time. It's amazing how items can disappear when tensions run high.

> *"My ex left me with a very challenging financial situation. The only assets I had were some art, furniture, and a car. He came in and took the art and furniture – but my lawyer helped me keep possession of the car so I could sell it to pay the mortgage."*

Investments. Outside of your house, your investments are probably your next biggest asset to deal with. The good news is that splitting investments is fairly straightforward in the eyes of the law. Here are some basic rules to get your started:

- **RRSPs and RRIFs** are considered family property, to be divided 50/50 in a legal separation or divorce. Spousal RRSPs are treated the same way.
- **Non-registered accounts** are also deemed family property and should be split the same way.
- **Pensions are property,** and their calculations are extremely complicated, so get your lawyer and/or your accountant to help with this. Depending on your situation and the province you live in, you (or your ex) may be entitled to up to 50% of the other's pension or vice versa. Rules in Ontario, for example, have recently been amended so that the receiving person doesn't have to wait until the giving person retires.

Life Insurance. Does your ex have a life insurance policy? He should. It's imperative that support gets paid if your ex passes away.

- Do you have your own policy? It's also fair, even if you aren't paying the majority of support, that your ex gets some help raising the children if you pass away.
- Does the policy amount cover your mortgage and your children's future education?
- Does the policy term match the approximate duration of support?

DEBT

Of all the financial subjects, this one may be the most stressful. If you have any joint credit cards, now is the time to cancel them or lower their credit limits in case your ex starts making big purchases that you might have to pay for. Reducing your line of credit limit and limits on other borrowing tools is also a must. And you'll need to discuss with your lawyer how to get an agreement in place on how any credit cards will be used between you and your ex going forward.

Regardless of whether it's your debt, his debt, or debt incurred by both of you, you should be putting all the documents you can get your hands on into a file folder. Before you do this, open up another worksheet in your spreadsheet document, call it "Debt," and begin to record your list of debt. This could include mortgages, credit cards, lines of credit, etc.

> *"What worked for me was being realistic and honest about my proposed budget. In some cases though, I was estimating lower than I should have. When that happened my lawyer suggested a more appropriate number."*

COMPLEX CHOICES, DIFFICULT DECISIONS

At this point, you are well aware that dealing with the finances doesn't end with filling in your financial statement. It involves a lot of complex choices, difficult decisions, good planning, and some emotional moments.

These decisions and this planning often take time to figure out and involve communication with friends, family, and hopefully, a financial advisor. Then there's the matter of actually coming to an agreement on all these issues with your ex.

Matrimonial home — to sell or stay?

Your home is probably your largest financial responsibility. Being able to sustain mortgage payments and general upkeep of the matrimonial home throughout the divorce process and beyond will be one of your toughest challenges.

> *"The first thing my dad said to me when I told him we were separating was, 'You have to sell your house.' I was so upset because I had just had a baby and couldn't think about uprooting our life that way. In the end, it was sage advice, and I am glad I took it. It helped move the process forward and get me settled into my new reality."*

> *"I spent a lot of time and emotional energy deliberating over whether or not to sell the house, unsure that I could afford it all on my own and manage all of the responsibility alone as well. In my case, my work situation changed shortly after I took over the house, which added great financial stress."*

Here are some questions to ask yourself as you make this decision:

- Can I ultimately afford to stay in the house? Will I be stressed every month to make the mortgage payment?
- Is relying on my ex to make regular and complete support payments realistic?
- Will moving cost more financially and emotionally than staying?
- What other costs beyond the mortgage payments do I need to consider?
- What impact will selling the house have on the children?

> ### SIX THINGS YOU NEED KNOW ABOUT YOUR MATRIMONIAL HOME
>
> **You both have a right to stay** in the home unless a judge deems otherwise (in the case of violence, abusive behaviour, or any safety concerns).
>
> **You split the proceeds** of the house 50/50, no matter whose name is on the title.
>
> **Neither of you would lose** the above rights if you were to move out of the house temporarily.
>
> **One spouse can't rent**, sublet, sell, or mortgage the matrimonial home without the other spouse's permission. In most cases, you will need your spouse's signature to sell your house, even if it is in your name.
>
> **A vacation property** can also be considered a matrimonial home (if it meets certain criteria).
>
> **You can apply for a removal order** if you want your ex out of your matrimonial home but you need good reason.

Simple math forces many divorcing couples to sell their homes. If you think you may need to sell your home, here are some tips to help you get started:

- Start getting real estate agent referrals and meet with agents to learn how they would approach selling your house.
- Figure out your timeline and the best time to sell.
- Meet with a financial planner to determine what you can afford to buy or rent.
- List your must-haves and nice-to-haves for a new home, and share it with your agent.

- Talk through this important decision with your therapist or your support network.

"Try to accept the idea of selling your home as soon as possible, especially if this decision will greatly decrease your financial stress."

Furniture — it's just stuff. Although furniture is technically "matrimonial property," don't cling to it — there are far more important things in life than "stuff."

- **Get help.** Tap your organizational expert to help you go through everything in the house for "must-keeps."
- **Let it go.** Try to unload as much stuff as you can. The less you have to move, the better.
- **Reach out.** Try to sell as much as you can online, through your network, or at a garage sale.
- **Sell, don't store.** You may have an urge to store bigger items in a facility, but the cost and hassle may not be worth it — make a decision early in the process.

Splitting up your stuff is a challenging task. There will be high emotions attached to various items in your home, and going through your stuff with your ex can be difficult.

- **Do it online.** One of you go through everything, make a list with a check beside each item you would like to keep, and go from there. It won't prevent squabbling, but it will be less noisy!

- **Choose the right time.** If you meet at the matrimonial home, don't do it too early in the process or during a tough week. This can make the whole thing go sideways. Make sure you are both ready for this long, possibly difficult, meeting.

- **Be fair.** It's hard to trade one-for-one with some objects, but, where you can, try to make it simple and even. The early, small concessions you make can pay great dividends down the road.

- **Stick to your guns.** Don't let your ex bully you and start taking things out of the house without a discussion. Even if you don't want something, make a point to discuss and document it — you can use that later for leverage/bargaining.

EQUALIZATION PAYMENTS

The household assets accumulated during a marriage still need to be equalized between the two parties in some fashion. This is generally done through an equalization payment calculation.

Not everyone is entitled to an equalization payment. For example, if both party's balance sheets end up the same, there is no equalization payment.

> ### EQUALIZATION PAYMENT
>
> A payment based on a calculation that determines how much money the person whose net asset value has increased most during the marriage should pay to the other so that they each end up with assets of equal value for the period of their marriage.

Equalization calculations are complicated and should be put in your lawyer's hands. They are the experts in this and have various software applications and tools at their disposal.

> *"The financial equalization theories and application of them while sometimes seemed logical ... got confusing."*

> *"Calculating equalization requires both parties to provide full financial disclosure. I spent one year in the courts trying to get my ex to provide that — to no avail ... in that case the judge simply imputed [determined] an income to/for my ex on which we based the calculation."*

THE IMPORTANCE OF A WILL

An important step not to forget is to update your will. Get a lawyer to draw up your will so that significant issues, such as power of attorney and guardianship, are accurately expressed and legally sound.

Make sure your will deals with family property, including pensions, RRSPs, and life insurance.

YOUR FINANCIAL RESET

As you split up your household assets, you may find that rebuilding your new independent life (while paying your legal bills) is challenging. This is something you will have to work to overcome with the help of your "A-team" — your financial advisor, knowledgeable family members or friends, and your lawyer.

> *"Getting divorced really messes up your retirement plan."*

> *"Just managing everything on one income, there is an adjustment period."*

> *"The most challenging aspect of the finances was doing it on my own, with two small children, while managing the house."*

The other aspect of your new financial life is that you can't necessarily rely on things like your ex's income to stay the same. It is common to review each party's finances annually. If your ex's income goes down, so might your support payments.

> *"He lost his high-paying job and then got a lower-paying job. I did not expect that to happen when I was negotiating the agreement. It happened many years later."*

> *"He lost his job and I got zero child support for four months. When he got another job [the salary] was half the previous amount. I did not think about that when I was negotiating the separation agreement."*

The reality is that women tend to have a bigger decrease in income than men post-divorce.

> "When things became very tight for me financially, I relied on a line of credit for a while to alleviate the stress of covering my monthly bills and expenses, feeling that I would worry about my debt when things settled down a bit (especially emotionally). I refinanced the house later on and paid off the line of credit."

> "I set up a line of credit before starting the divorce process, but I underestimated the cost of my legal fees. If you are setting up a line of credit, go big and if you do not use it, that's a bonus."

While this sentiment is grim, all of the women surveyed for this book found a way to make things work financially — and they learned a lot in the process.

Spending the time, effort, and energy making realistic financial decisions is an important part of moving forward. By calling on the expertise of your professional team, you will reduce your stress and regain confidence in your financial decision-making skills.

8 SUPPORT: AGREEING ON IT AND GETTING IT

AGREEING ON IT

> *"Financials are very, very subjective, and it became increasingly clear to me just how easy it was to manipulate numbers and change the perception."*

While many people are able to work co-operatively to arrive at a fair support amount and pay regular and complete support payments, this was a main source of frustration for this book's contributors. The frustration was two-fold: firstly, agreeing on it, and secondly, actually getting it. This is one of the most stressful aspects of divorce because the amount of support received and/or paid has a definite impact on your future.

Lawyers and judges rely on certified software applications to calculate spousal and/or child support. However, our contributors found that was an area riddled with grey areas, myths, and questionable behaviour. Here are just a few:

Income minimization

> *"My ex continually stated a lower income on his financial statement and then refused to provide supporting documentation to prove it."*

Hiding income

> "My ex-husband has a portion of his income that is derived from consulting. He has been neither forthcoming nor credible in reporting his true income."

Earning cash

> "My ex-husband does work for cash so his income is not transparent for the purpose of determining support."

Using loopholes

> "My ex got incorporated two months after I left. He has a lot of bogus expenses that bring down his income. We have yet to tackle this."

Not factoring in bonuses

> "I was confused about money beyond salary (i.e., shares, bonuses, and stock options). My ex-husband told me that he only had to pay child support based on his 'salary.' So he underpaid me child support for several years."

Improper financial disclosure is one of the major reasons this part of the divorce process is contentious. Hope for honesty and partnership, but be aware of potential games. Your lawyer will be able to identify these quickly.

> "I had sole custody, and my ex refused to provide proper financial disclosure for more than two years. We kept going back to court, and he kept getting chances to provide his financials ... which he never did."

SPOUSAL SUPPORT

Spousal support can be complicated because it's based on the spousal support advisory guidelines that are just that: guidelines; they have not been legislated.

> **SPOUSAL SUPPORT: QUICK FACTS**
>
> Spousal support is the amount a spouse is required to pay for the period of time necessary for the lower-income spouse to become economically self-sufficient.
>
> - Spousal support is taxable
> - Not everyone gets spousal support
> - It can be set for a particular amount of time
> - Women and men are both eligible

These guidelines are helpful in giving estimates on the numbers, but they do NOT determine what a spouse is entitled to in terms of support. The reality is you, your ex, and your legal resources will come to an agreement on this or the courts will decide for you.

> *"The fact that spousal support is not a legislated amount is a huge stumbling block for many people. Hopefully it will become a legislated amount like child support."*

Here are the factors that will affect the decided-upon amount:

- Age and health.
- The financial means and needs of both spouses.
- The standard of living pre-separation.
- Available employment.
- The length of the marriage (someone married for twenty years who was looking after the children would likely seek more spousal support than someone married for five years who worked throughout the marriage).
- The role each spouse played (including caregiving) during the marriage.
- The amount of time needed to become "self-sufficient."
- The ongoing care and needs of the children.

CHILD SUPPORT

Unlike spousal support, there are legislated tables for child support. Child support is calculated in two ways:

1. A basic amount calculated using the Child Support Tables.
2. Section 7 expenses (outlined below) — additional expenses like tuition, extra-curricular activities, or equipment.

> ### CHILD SUPPORT
>
> Periodic payments payable by a non-custodial parent to the custodial parent for the care of his or her child.

Child Support Tables
Calculating child support is based on:
- Custody
- The payer's and payee's incomes
- How many children are involved
- The decided-upon parenting arrangement

Child support tables are readily available online. Do some research to get familiar with them but remember this is just a starting point. The formula for calculating child support also includes Section 7 expenses (outlined below).

> *"When I first started the process, I went online and found a calculator to help me get a sense of what child support might look like. I found the numbers to be shockingly low and started to panic — how could I possibly raise my son on this? My lawyer explained Section 7 expenses, and we worked through several scenarios that got me to a more realistic number."*

What are Section 7 expenses?

Section 7 expenses are calculated proportionally based on you and your ex's stated incomes. These are expenses that are too costly for the asking parent to pay given that person's income, including child support. However, these are expenses that must be an amount that the paying parent can reasonably afford. Section 7 expenses may include:

- Childcare expenses for when you are legitimately unable to care for your children full-time (e.g., illness, work).
- Healthcare needs beyond what insurance covers (e.g., orthodontics, dental work).
- A portion of health insurance premiums that cover children.
- Primary and secondary education, as well as tutoring.
- The child's expenses for post-secondary education.
- Extra-curricular activities including after-school programs, trips, and camps.

There are many factors regarding extra-curricular activities that need to be considered, including:

- How many programs the kids are participating in.
- The costs of these programs.
- The importance of the activity to the kids.

SIX IMPORTANT FACTS ABOUT CHILD SUPPORT

Child support is not taxable (although spousal support is).

Child Support Tables are not indexed by geography, so the cost of living in different cities or towns isn't accounted for.

The age of majority is either 18 or 19 depending on the province in which you reside. This will impact

> the number of years parents must legally support their children.
>
> **Child support continues after 18** if the child is enrolled in a full-time educational program.
>
> **Bankruptcy** does not negate support.
>
> **Priority must be given to child support** when a person applies for both child and spousal support.
>
> **You get a tax credit for legal fees** relating to child support issues. Keep these bills for tax time.

WHEN YOU EARN MORE THAN YOUR EX

If you earn more than your ex, you may find yourself in a frustrating situation. The law implicitly assumes that the partner who earns less money is the woman. It goes on to assume that in a family with children, the woman functioned as the primary caregiver and may have sacrificed her career for the family. As a result, women who earn more than their spouses but who also took on more of the household and child-rearing tasks can get penalized for their hyper-efficiency.

A woman can get stuck supporting an ex indefinitely, even if he was working when the separation took place and he initiated the separation.

> *"As the primary bread-winner in our family, I felt that the system was biased against me. The system assumes that the parent who earns less probably contributed equally or more to parenting. In my case, I earned more, worked more, and was the primary parent. These facts were irrelevant, except that I was in a position to pay significant amounts of spousal support to my ex."*

ANNUAL REVIEW

Once you have an agreement in place, you will likely review your financial circumstances (including support) every year. As your life and/or your children's lives change and evolve, you may find that you need to redefine the terms of your support.

> "When they are in Grade 1, you have no idea how much they will cost when they are teens!!! Especially boys. And then there is the fact that if your ex used to make $80,000 and lost his job, you would get $0. And if he got another job at a much lower rate, like $35,000, you would just get the table amount! I have the children 68% of the time and they are sixteen and eighteen years old, and I get $525 a month. This barely feeds them for a week!"

> "I do have to push very hard every year to have my ex review the support amount and have him adjust it. Every year, the month that he does this gets later and later. Recently, he has maintained my monthly support at the same level, but he provides me with the difference in an end-of-the-year lump-sum payment when he receives his bonus."

GETTING SUPPORT PAID ... OR NOT

Support can be paid:
- By cash, cheque, or money order.
- By government-run Maintenance Enforcement Programs (MEPs).
- By wage garnishment.

Many people are paid (or pay) support by cheque or through transferring money into a joint account. However, a growing number of people have to deal with late or light payments. And in a few cases, an ex pays no support at all. In 2012, Statistics Canada estimated that 45% of child and spousal support orders were in arrears.

> "My ex-husband simply decided not to pay support — and for two years there was nothing I could do about it except wait for the courts to get annoyed enough to do something about it."
>
> "Fighting for child support is constant — I certainly did not realize that child support would be an ongoing issue. You have to always fight to get it. The fact that I have to keep going back to court to get basic things like child support enforced (while he continues to live a very lavish life) is completely absurd!"
>
> "I thought my ex would help with the children. In seven years, he has not paid for a haircut, pair of shoes, school program, school trip, health insurance, gift, prescription, etc. I could go on. The list does not end."

While it's true that you need to pick your battles, child support shouldn't be one that you back off on. Single-handedly paying for your children's expenses is ridiculous. Make sure you keep your lawyer informed and keep track of your expenses in a budget.

MAINTENANCE ENFORCEMENT PROGRAMS

> "My ex claimed personal bankruptcy to get out of paying support. It didn't negate him from paying support, but it certainly slowed the process down."

In Canada, Maintenance Enforcement Programs (MEPs) help manage and enforce payments and enforce private separation agreements.

MAINTENANCE ENFORCEMENT PROGRAM

A provincial or territorial body that can help enforce your registered support order or written agreement. MEPs are able to initiate enforcement action with a temporary or interim order.

MEPs have been established in all provinces and territories to assist in getting support obligations fulfilled. These programs have slight differences, but they are all supported by federal laws that allow decisive action to be taken against those who don't pay support.

Here are some enforcement actions available to MEPs:

- Notify employers about a non-compliant spouse's behaviour.
- Report behaviour to the credit bureau or other professional or occupational organizations.
- Garnishee bank accounts or federal money (e.g., income tax refunds, employment insurance benefits, CPP, and OAS).
- Suspend driver's license.
- Suspend passport.
- Place a lien against the house, other real estate, or other personal property, which means if it is sold or refinanced, the proceeds will be directed to pay the seller's debt.
- Issue a writ against payer's property, which is a court order giving enforcement officers the authority to seize and sell a debtor's property.
- Seize lottery winnings.
- Start a default hearing (which could result in up to 180 days of jail time).

> *"My ex-husband pays me spousal support. He often claims to be confused on the amount. I finally decided to use the MEP to enforce payment."*

Using a MEP as your path to payment may be long and difficult. If you suspect that your ex will not pay support, engage your lawyer early on to see when you can start a case file with your provincial MEP.

To start a case file you will need to:
- Provide all court orders relating to the details of your support order.
- Complete a case form and history of payments.
- Get the document notarized.

BE YOUR OWN ADVOCATE

> *"I called my MEP caseworker every month for an update. After a few months, I realized enforcement had stalled, and I kept getting the same update. I had to make a formal complaint and get my Member of Provincial Parliament to write a letter before anything moved forward."*

Once you are in a MEP system your legal bills will decrease, as your lawyer will be doing less (they typically don't play a role in the MEP process), but you will be doing more — you need to be your own advocate when it comes to MEPs.

MEPs can be bureaucratic and slow. You will have to dedicate time and energy to staying on top of your case. Here are some ideas:

- Build a relationship with your case officer.
- Put a date in your calendar to call every month for an update.
- Keep a file containing all copies of any paperwork you have submitted.
- Make sure your financial statement is accurate and up to date.
- Keep a log of every communication including the date of the conversation, arrears to date, dates of any enforcement actions, and dates of any proposed timelines or actions.

Support is one of the most stress-inducing parts of divorce. It brings out everyone's biggest fears and anxieties. It can turn you into your worst self. However, through education and learning to advocate for yourself you can take back a little control and start to feel stronger.

9 CUSTODY, ACCESS, & PARENTING: FINDING THE RIGHT SOLUTION

JOINT, SHARED, SPLIT, OR SOLE?

> *"You will spend a lot of time explaining to people (whether you like it or not) the differences between custody and access."*

It's not surprising there is this confusion of meaning: there are a lot of custody-related terms, and sometimes there are several names for the same situation. For example, full custody and sole custody are the same thing, but joint custody and shared custody are not.

Legal custody vs. physical custody. Legal custody refers to who makes the major decisions on a child's behalf regarding:

- Education
- Religion
- Health and welfare

Physical custody refers to whom the children live with. It's not necessarily the same person as the one who has legal custody.

Sole custody (or full custody). A sole- or full-custody parent has both legal custody (decision-making) and physical custody (caregiving) for the kids.

The other parent, the one without sole custody, has visitation rights, which are the same as access rights, and can have knowledge about the major decisions being made, but has no legal custody.

> *"There is also the issue of your ex saving face. No guy wants to go around saying he doesn't have custody of his children, so this will always become a contentious issue. Trying to get sole custody means a long road in the court system."*

It's not easy to get sole custody in Canada, particularly if your ex doesn't want this. Judges take this issue very seriously. It will take time and substantial evidence before this decision gets made.

Joint vs. shared. Joint custody refers to legal custody, and it means that both parents make joint decisions regarding education, religion, and health and welfare. A couple can agree on joint custody (also known as joint legal custody) even if only one parent has physical custody.

Shared custody can also be called joint physical custody and refers to physical custody. It means the children live at least 40% of the time with each parent annually. Many people think the divide has to be closer to 50/50, but this is not usually the case — one parent usually plays a greater role.

THE BENEFITS OF SHARED CUSTODY

Many studies have shown that conflict between parents can decrease over time, and co-operation can increase in a shared custody arrangement.

Split custody. Split custody is a situation in which each parent has custody of one or more of the children. One or more of the children lives with one parent more than 60% of the time annually, and one or more of the children lives with the other parent more than 60% of the time annually. For example, if the family was Mom, Dad, Jack, and Jill, Jill might live with Dad more than 60% of the time, and Jack with Mom more than 60% of the time.

Regardless of the custody model you are seeking, it's worth stating that this book's contributors all firmly believe there are three tenets to follow:

Children first. It is accepted knowledge that during divorce where kids are involved, one of the most important things is to put their interests first. In fact, parental acrimony during separation and divorce is highly correlated to children's perceived cognitive competence, and parental wars take a great toll on a child's development.[3]

> "It should be child first, child focused. Put aside your ego and your own needs. We have shared custody 50/50, week on and week off. What has really worked for me and my ex is that we have always considered where our son would get the most out of his life. You get back what you give; both from your child and from your ex."

Find opportunities in "alone time." The prospect of sharing your kids with your ex can be difficult to get your head around, but there are benefits. Most divorced women are the primary caregivers of their children, and many of them work full-time. You can use your alone time to do something for you!

> "Despite the extreme acrimony and pain of my divorce, I felt the complete legal and physical responsibility for my child was exhausting and stressful. I actually wished I had backing from my ex regarding our child's care and future."

---

[3] Daniel S. Shaw and Robert E. Emery, "Parental Conflict and Other Correlates of the Adjustment of School-Age Children Whose Parents Have Separated," *Journal of Abnormal Child Psychology*, 15(2) (1987): 269-281.

Maintain a relationship with your ex. In most cases, children need both their parents, and even if you are granted sole or full custody, you will likely still want a strong supporting parental presence in your children's lives.

> "I feel VERY strongly that if the father is a committed father, the children should be given a chance to have a real relationship with him that involves real parenting challenges. This decision involved me getting out of the way and really considering what was best for the children."

HOW ARE CUSTODY AND ACCESS DETERMINED?

> "Good, workable custody depends on the personalities involved and on the specifics of each family's situation. If you go through mediation, you can come up with a customized solution, but only if you can actually work effectively with your ex. On the other hand, the courts tend to provide a one-size-fits-all solution to problems that are never one-size-fits-all and don't accommodate for changes."

Your lawyer will help guide you, but, like most aspects of this process, you will need to think upfront about whether you want to take a lower-conflict, lower-cost approach (i.e., mediation) or go through the courts. And, again, this decision will come back to your assessment of your ex and what negotiation style suits you best.

Mediation is designed for two parties who are willing and able to negotiate, with both people wanting to participate in the decision-making process.

On the other hand, if you are in a stalemate situation, you will need to rely on the courts, and a decision will be made for you based on the evidence you and your ex provide.

This is what a judge considers when deciding on custody and parenting arrangements:

- The relationship that the children have with each parent.

- Childcare arrangements before the separation.
- The children's age and needs.
- Each parent's abilities.
- The parents' abilities to get along and communicate effectively.
- Safety.

Before making a decision, a judge will frequently recommend that both parties utilize a third-party parenting co-ordinator to provide a recommendation back to the court. This process can take many months, and sometimes, due to scheduling, up to a year or more.

Safety is a factor. Your children's safety is a primary consideration when it comes to custody. If your ex is not competent and still fights to be your children's sole custodian, ask yourself:

- Can my ex put my children's interests first all the time?
- Can my ex maintain emotional stability?

If the answer is no to both, you could look at having a Parenting Capacity Assessment (PCA) done.

PARENTING CAPACITY ASSESSMENT

A psychological examination to determine parental fitness.

If you are truly concerned about your ex's parenting skills (and hence your children's safety), your lawyers can file a motion for a PCA. You, your ex, and even your children will be interviewed several times by a social worker, psychologist, and/or psychiatrist, and a report will be drawn up.

The cost of a PCA, which focuses mainly on the needs of the children, is usually split between you and your ex. The assessment can cost approximately $8,000 to $10,000 (or more) and can take from three months to a year to complete.

ACCESS AND PARENTING PLANS

Regardless of the custody arrangement, every parent has the right to access his or her child. You will need to agree on an access or visitation schedule that works for both parties, and it will be clearly documented in your separation agreement. You can use your lawyer or a parenting co-ordinator to architect your plan.

ACCESS IS NOT TIED TO SUPPORT

It's a very common misperception that access and support are somehow linked; they are not. Many women receive inappropriate or no support payments from their ex, but still have to (and want to) establish and maintain a visitation schedule.

The most common arrangement consists of a split schedule during weekdays and weekends to give as close to equal access as possible to each parent.

> *"I would definitely recommend that the parenting plan/terms of access be as specific as possible."*

A less common arrangement is supervised access and typically occurs if there are safety concerns.

SUPERVISED ACCESS

If one parent has sole custody, there are some cases where supervised custody is warranted. In very serious cases, a social worker is appointed to supervise visitations in a neutral place (not your home). In other cases, a separation agreement can stipulate that a parent, grandparent, or caregiver be present during access visits.

A best practice is to develop a parenting plan that lays out your schedule and how day-to-day decisions are made and communicated. The main thing to keep in mind when creating a parenting plan is to negotiate something that works for you and your kids. The plan you decide on is something you are going to have to live with, so be sure to set out your objectives and make sure you are happy with these objectives.

Parenting plans typically cover:
- Daytime and evening schedules.
- Holidays.
- Each of your living arrangements and locations.
- Childcare options.
- Movement from home to home.
- Extra-curricular activities.
- Communication, whether it be email, phone, or text.
- Management of clothes and other belongings.
- Rules of engagement between you and your ex, and the process for escalation should there be a stalemate.
- Regular meeting and review times.

It remains important for your ex to develop and maintain a relationship with your children in whatever capacity possible. Your best tool is a clear and specific separation agreement.

CO-PARENTING: RULES OF THE ROAD

The initial transition period of "sharing" your children takes some getting used to. Doing it well takes some serious organization and communication skills. It also requires a great deal of co-operation between you and your ex. If you can work through the challenges of calmly planning holidays, dental appointments, and extra-curricular activities with your ex, you will have the optimal post-divorce family arrangement. Here are some tips:

Stick to the schedule.
- Do your best to stick to this schedule. It's not in your best interest (or your child's) to be changing plans on the fly.

- If your ex is unreliable and tries to change days, make surprise visits, bank days for later, or make up missed days at a time that is not convenient, put your foot down. Your child's schedule is paramount. Don't hesitate to pull out and review the schedule you and your ex both signed and paid for as a reminder.
- Divide your schedule into specific "time of the year" categories to eliminate unknowns and give yourself a blueprint for unique circumstances:
  - School/routine days
  - Weekends
  - Summer
  - Holidays

"Think long-term and be a united front as co-parents. I've seen children who suffer during the teen years because one parent gives into a child's desire to stay with a parent who either has more "stuff" or provides more freedom. As co-parents, we've talked about always supporting each other whenever the children are concerned to make sure they understand that our arrangement is non-negotiable. While it might be a drag to live in two homes as a teenager, it will be their reality. A firm plan not only benefits the co-parents, but also the children."

Get into the details.

- Map out everything from Christmas to Passover to Halloween, from soccer games to family birthdays. The more you stick to the agreed-upon arrangements, the better off you'll all be.
- Iron out even the smallest details. Who is picking up? Who is dropping off? Will you be at school concerts together? Have you made time for the grandparents?

"It's been over six years since my divorce and, for the most part, things have been smooth re: co-parenting. Our primary challenges are when one parent signs our child up for extra-curricular activities that require the other parent's involvement (e.g., dance that requires the other parent to travel). While changes to the co-parenting schedule/plan can be irritating, this hasn't caused us major grief, as the activity is one that our daughter really enjoys."

"The easiest way to get all the details documented is to talk through each scenario and get every last detail on the table — it will save you stress in the long run."

Include your children.
- Keep a large, visible calendar in a central place so your children know where they will be and who they will be with at all times.

"I was worried about how my kids would manage with living between two different houses. I got them to help build-out our parenting calendar: writing the dates they were at my house and the dates they were at their dad's. I think it helped them feel like part of the process, which made the transition easier."

Communicate.
- Try to give your ex as much information as possible. Keep your ex in the loop on day-to-day issues and always give him or her a chance to be involved in decision-making as it relates to the children. If you don't want to speak regularly, implement a weekly check-in schedule where you reconnect and update one another about the children's schedule.
- Don't rely on your children to make plans with their parent on their own.
- Use email as often as possible so you have a paper trail to check in case of miscommunication.
- Try as much as possible to give each other a week's notice when there are changes required.
- Use tools like Google Calendar for easy information sharing and instant updates on your mobile device.

"We started communicating by email on a weekly basis — that was easiest for me. After keeping this regular pattern of communication up, we were eventually able to make plans on the phone and even in person."

Develop rules about the phone and contact.
- Make sure your separation agreement includes how you want to manage communication, especially phone conversations, when the parent without the children wants to make contact, or the children want to contact that parent.

"When my ex lived away, open phone access and some privacy for my son's calls with his dad was important."

"When it comes to older children, it may be difficult to keep your ex happy with the amount that the children are contacting your ex (teenagers are typically in their own world), so it takes extra effort on your part to remind your child to make contact."

Be flexible.
- Respect that the schedule can be changed for special events, visiting family members, last-minute tickets to a hockey game, and illness or work emergencies.
- Be flexible where you can, and expect flexibility in return.

"My ex is very controlling and, for example, restricts my children's access to the telephone. He is also very strict about me not seeing my children when it is not my week unless there is some "official" event. I try to stay on the high road."

Don't try to do it all.
- If your ex is willing to pitch in beyond what you've agreed on, go for it.
- Ask for help when you need it with specific tasks.

"It took me time to rebuild some trust with my ex, but once I did, I found that he could be a good resource to take the kids out and give me time to get my errands done."

Be civil.
- Don't let your personal spite prevent your children from seeing their parent.

- It's not always easy, but try to use kindness and consideration to set the tone for the future.
- Try not to work out your relationship issues through the children.

"Avoid criticizing each other's parenting style, but try to co-operate and work together to be consistent in areas where there is agreement. I find that it's hard sometimes not to let my needs and my issues creep into my negotiations with my ex, but it's always better when I don't."

CARDINAL RULE #1

Never bad-mouth your ex to your children.

Be aware of stages and changes.
- On the one hand, it's important that once you've decided on your custody arrangement that you stick with it, at least for a while. Children play parents off each other (even in non-divorced families). They simply may want to avoid chores or stick around for a "fun" week. That said, there may come a time when your child will choose to spend more time with one of you, and this is his or her right from the age of around twelve, depending on the child's maturity level.

- As children turn into teens, they start to want to control their lives a bit more. This is normal and healthy since, by the age of eighteen, they may be living on their own. Parents should be encouraging their teens to be independent whenever possible. Allowing teens a voice in living arrangements makes sense in this context. At this point in the parenting process, it is more important to think about what is best for the teen than what either parent would ideally like to see happen. We need to let go of the idea that living arrangements are about us — the parents — and our conflicts.

However messy and painful co-parenting can be, you can be successful. Consider yourself successful if, as a co-parent, you have:

- Fostered a relationship between your children and their other parent.
- Reduced conflict between yourself and your ex.
- Provided a peaceful, positive environment for your children.

"I think my ex-husband's relationship with his children has been strengthened by the solo time spent with his children. I also think I've forged a tremendous bond with my children as a result of our time together."

"My victory is to have survived it and thrived, and to see my children happy, healthy, and having a good relationship with their father. Success is moving on in an emotionally healthy way where children can feel and sense peace between parents."

"Success to me is when my ex and I were able to have a civil conversation about our children without any animosity or meanness. We never put our children in a position to be played back and forth between us."

THE REALITIES OF SOLE CUSTODY

While getting sole custody may feel like a win, the reality is that sole custody is exhausting. Being your child's full-time caregiver, organizer, and emotional support while working full-time, dealing with your divorce, and trying to rebuild your life leaves you very little time for yourself. If sole custody is your reality, put some of these things in place:

- **Carefully select a close support network.** In the case of sole custody, having a solid team around you is imperative. This team could include family, friends, a babysitter/nanny, or a trustworthy next-door neighbour. Make sure you let these people know they are part of your network and set the expectation that you may rely on them from time to time.

"I am lucky to have my parents and brother in the same city — I especially rely on my Mum. I couldn't have done this without her."

- **Make sure you take a break.** Learn to identify when you are at your limit, and, if possible, set up scheduled breaks in advance. It's easy to let your personal time slide if you don't have anything established.

    "I make a point of taking a break once a quarter — it could be twenty-four hours to myself or a weekend away. I always feel rejuvenated and believe I can be a better parent afterwards."

- **Don't feel guilty.** You need to be the best you can be for your children, and that means taking care of yourself too.

    "I feel guilty because my daughter has such a dysfunctional father, and I find myself trying to compensate for that — and feeling guilty when I do something for myself and not her. I know it's wrong, but I think it's the curse of a parent with sole custody."

The bottom line is that sole custody is a lot of work, but with the right supports in place and the occasional break, it can be done successfully for you and your children.

Custody and parenting models continuously evolve as work and personal lives change. This chapter outlines the more standard models, but don't be constrained by these alone. The key is to build a model that truly works for you, your ex, and your children. And if you find it's not working, raise your hand, make some adjustments, and test it out. Your mental state will thank you.

10 LIFE AFTER THE DIVORCE: BREAKING FROM THE PAST

YOUR CHALLENGE AS A DIVORCED WOMAN

> *"I was the primary caregiver with sole custody; my ex paid NO support, and I was working full-time to pay for all my daughter's needs."*

It's sad but true: on average, women pull a heavier load when it comes to family relationships (including divorce) than men do. Even an amicable divorce with joint custody can result in a greater emotional workload for the woman.

Judith Wallerstein, a psychologist and researcher who created a twenty-five-year study on the effects of divorce found that 90% of divorced women became the primary caregiver for their children.

What's more, 74% of the divorced women in the study experienced a reduced socioeconomic status, while only 42% of divorced men did.[4]

The bottom line is that while there are many couples that co-ordinate their activities to achieve a shared balance of childcare, women often

---

[4] Second Chances: Men, Women and Children a Decade After Divorce, Judith Wallerstein with Sandra Blakeslee, Ticknor & Fields, 1989

carry more of the responsibility for planning, enforcing visits, and monitoring the other parent in divorced families. Try to avoid falling into this trap if you can. Take time for yourself. Offload some parenting and planning responsibility onto your ex. Don't allow your energy, talents, and productivity to be sapped by the divorce process by taking on an outsized workload. Try to push back, just a little, and maybe the balance could tip the scales a little more in your favour. Children need two happy, productive parents. Do what you need to do to be your best post-divorce self.

YOUR POST-DIVORCE TEAM

After you're finally divorced, you're probably still going to want a team to help you stay happy and healthy. Your team might include some of the following:

Family therapist

Make sure that all is okay with your kid(s) and your different family unit(s) as they settle into their new post-divorce reality. For children, in particular, a therapist acts as an objective listener who can help them work through their feelings about the divorce. Many children feel guilty and even responsible for their parents' divorce. Nip those destructive feelings in the bud and clear the air with one or two upbeat sessions with an experienced therapist.

Life coach

A certified life coach can help with organization, goal setting, and career planning — you decide what's missing and find a coach who suits your needs.

Personal trainer

Getting in shape and feeling great about the way you look and feel are two important ways to improve your self-esteem and get out there again.

And exercise-produced endorphins are one of the best and quickest ways to help you see things in a more positive light.

Other wellness professionals

This could be a yoga instructor, a massage therapist, nutritionist, naturopath, acupuncturist, or a meditation teacher. Getting involved in something that will help your body and mind is great, and you might just meet some like-minded, life-changing people.

STARTING OVER

Even if you are still hurting from your divorce, recognize that you have the right to move forward, to grow, heal, and plan for your own future. You can get back on track. Better yet, you can get on a new track.

> *"Once I decided that he was not part of my personal life anymore, it felt empowering. You protect yourself once you are ready to decide that he is not part of who you are anymore. You will deal with him for the rest of your life regarding the children, but he is not part of your life and that is the difference."*

As you start your life as a single person, you have the chance to reinvent yourself, or parts of yourself, in ways that reflect the new you.

Rebuild your personal network

You have your inner circle of friends and family whom you can rely on, but they can't be your only source of interaction. You need to start developing a new personal network to help you move forward.

Let your inner circle know when you are ready to start going out and living life again. Whether it's going to social events, movies, sports games, theatre, or concerts — you are game! Get a sitter and get out of the house.

> *"I found the more I got out, the more people I met, which helped me adopt a more positive attitude. The world didn't seem so heavy."*

Rewrite your story

When meeting new people, it's easy to lead with what is likely preoccupying your thoughts — your divorce. Try to avoid this if possible. Your new network is not your old life.

> "My impulse was to let people know I was a struggling single mother who didn't receive child support. The whole thing didn't seem fair, and I wanted to share that with the people I met. But I realized that saying it was making me live through a little piece of it every time, which wasn't good (or really that interesting to anyone!)."

Developing your new network isn't going to happen overnight. Try new things and be open to new opportunities you never would have tried before — like a new sport, language, or a book club — or groups of people or activities you've avoided because your ex didn't like them.

> "I had to learn to reconnect as my 'new self.' It took practice, but I ended up developing some really rewarding relationships with people whom I would have never been exposed to in my past life."

HOW TO FIT YOUR EX INTO YOUR NEW LIFE

If you have children, your ex will be a part of your life for many years to come. As you rediscover who you are post-divorce, you will need to continually fine-tune your interactions with your ex to protect your new self and to keep things amicable. It may be difficult but remember that you are no longer married to him, and that a calm, civil conversation always works best. You can only control what you do, so focus on managing your own behaviour.

> "I need to be very calm and collected. If I've had a stressful day that has left me frazzled, it is very unlikely that the conversation with my ex will go well."

Taking the high road isn't always the easy option, but it will always serve you well in the end. When you are feeling positive, people sense it. Your behaviour influences how others perceive you and how they interact with you and will always help you achieve the positive outcome you want. Set your personal goals, and move forward with what you need. Today is a new day!

CONCLUSION: YOUR LIFE AHEAD OF YOU

If you're reading this book just as you're about to start the process of getting divorced, you're probably in a pretty dark place. All of the women interviewed for this book were once where you are. And now, after a few years of going through a process similar to what you're about to embark on, they have all (really, all!) found a new life socially, financially, and with their family.

It may seem far away from where you are right now, but please trust that you will get there too. I hope these last few thoughts from our contributors inspire you to believe this.

> *"When I look back at my divorce, it feels like a million years ago — and it was only five years ago. Time does heal all wounds."*

> *"I like the person I am today more than the one I was. I think the people around me do too. My divorce helped me find myself again. Today I am more confident, know myself better, and I'm happier."*

> *"If I could offer one piece of advice to any woman entering into the divorce process, it would be to be hopeful, patient, and open. Break down your walls and rebuild."*

"I learned so much about myself and other people during my divorce. I used the experience to evolve and become a better person, and that is the parent, wife, daughter, co-worker, and friend everyone sees today."

GLOSSARY

Access. The right of the parent with whom the child does not live to spend time with that child. Also known as visitation.

Affidavit. A written statement voluntarily made under oath, which provides facts that could be of consequence in court.

Applicant. The person who files for divorce. This is done using a general application.

Arbitration. A dispute resolution process in which the parties hire a neutral third party (in the case of divorce, a family law arbitrator) to make a decision that resolves their dispute, which they agree to be bound by. The arbitrator's job is to act like a judge and impose a resolution after hearing the evidence and listening to the arguments of each party.

Case conference. An official meeting with the two exes, their lawyers, and a judge, with the goal of identifying issues that the parties agree and disagree on. Also known as a settlement conference.

Co-parenting. The act of having both exes involved in the lives of their children. Most effective co-parenting arrangements include co-operation, communication, compromise, and consistency.

Custody. The responsibility to care for — and make decisions for — a child.

>   **Full custody.** See: Sole custody.

>   **Joint custody.** The parents share decision-making about the child. The child may live mostly with one parent, spend equal time with both parents, or a number of other different scenarios.

> **Shared custody.** The child spends at least 40% of his or her time with each parent every year.
>
> **Sole custody.** The child lives with one parent and visits with the other. The custodial parent is responsible for all major decisions affecting the child. The other parent should be consulted about major decisions and usually has the right to receive information about the child's health, education, and welfare. A parent who has sole custody has both legal custody and physical custody. It is very rare for a parent to get sole custody in Canada today. Also known as full custody.
>
> **Split custody.** Each parent has at least one child living with him or her.
>
> **Legal custody.** This refers to the parent who makes the major decisions on a child's behalf regarding education, religion, health, and welfare.
>
> **Physical custody.** This refers to whom a child lives with. It's not necessarily the same person as the one who has legal custody.

Divorce. The legal end to a marriage.

Equalization payment. A payment, based on a calculation, that determines how much money the person whose net asset value has increased most during the marriage should pay to the other so they each end up with assets of equal value for the period of their marriage.

Examination for discovery. See: Questioning.

Factum. A short document concisely summarizing an argument. It may include a list of relevant case law to support the argument.

Financial statement. A sworn document that includes a statement of income, other assets and liabilities, and other information that might be relevant to support (such as special or extraordinary expenses).

Hearing. The presentation of evidence before an adjudicating body.

> **Motion hearing.** A legal proceeding in which both sides can present their arguments while providing factual evidence. These are typically more limited in scope than trials.

Pre-trial hearing. The occasion when the parties identify the actual issues for trial. Orders and directions may be obtained in a pre-trial hearing so that the trial will proceed more efficiently.

Maintenance Enforcement Program. A provincial or territorial program that can help enforce an ex's registered support order or written agreement. These programs are able to initiate enforcement action — sometimes aggressively — with an interim order.

Matrimonial home. Every property in which a person has an interest and that is — or, if the spouses have been separated, was at the time of separation — ordinarily occupied by the person and his or her spouse as their family residence.

Matrimonial property. Any property or assets either spouse owns or obtains before or during the marriage. It doesn't matter whose name the property is in. All matrimonial property should be split 50/50 between the spouses if they separate or divorce, with some exceptions. Exceptions can include a gift or inheritance, insurance payout awarded to one spouse by a court, business assets (such as tools or a building), and property that was excluded in a pre-nuptial agreement.

Mediation. A form of alternative dispute resolution for resolving disputes between two or more parties with concrete effects. Typically a third party, the mediator (who can also be a lawyer but does not give legal advice), assists the parties in negotiating a settlement.

Motion. A written or oral application made to a court or judge to obtain a ruling or order directing that some act be done in favour of the motion applicant.

Order. A formal, written direction given by a member of the judiciary.

> **Court order.** An official proclamation by a judge. An order can be as simple as setting a date for trial or as complex as custody arrangements and support payment schedules.
>
> **Draft order.** An order drafted by a lawyer in advance of the motion hearing. It outlines the terms the lawyer's client is seeking.

Interim order. An official proclamation by a judge that is effective only for a limited time or until the final decision of the court. Also known as temporary order.

Temporary order. See: Interim order.

Parenting Capacity Assessment. A psychological examination to determine parental fitness.

Parenting co-ordinator. Experienced professionals — family law lawyers, counsellors, social workers, family therapists, or psychologists — who have special training in mediating and arbitrating parenting disputes in a child-focused way.

Parenting plan. A written document outlining how two exes are going to parent their children during the separation and afterwards. It usually covers where and with whom the children will live, which parent will make decisions relating to the children, what input or decision-making power the other parent will have, what contact the children will have with the parents, and anything else that is important to the child's welfare.

Questioning. A pre-trial occasion when a lawyer can ask questions of their client's ex, with the ex's lawyer present, to acquire new information and/or to confirm information they already have. Also known as examination for discovery.

Respondent. The person who responds to the general application.

Section 7 expenses. Expenses that lead one ex to request a higher amount of child support from the other ex than is outlined in the provincial guidelines. The expenses include tuition, extra-curricular activities, sports equipment, medical expenses, and more. Section 7 expenses are calculated proportionally based on your and your ex's stated incomes. Also known as special expenses.

Separation agreement. A written contract between two exes dealing with child custody, access, support payments, and the division of their property and debts. Also known as settlement agreement.

Settlement agreement. See: Separation agreement.

Settlement conference. See: Case conference.

Special expenses: See: Section 7 expenses.

Support. Money paid by one ex to the other for living expenses. Support is usually paid monthly, but can also be paid weekly, bi-weekly, or, in the case of spousal support, in a lump sum.

> **Child support.** Support for living expenses for a child or children. Usually not tax deductible.
>
> **Spousal support.** Support for the living expenses of an ex. Usually tax deductible.

Visitation. See: Access.

ABOUT THE AUTHOR

Jillian was inspired to write this book while going through a difficult divorce. Through her own experience, she felt there was no practical, single-source guide that easily explained the legal system and process, how to work with lawyers and your ex, or where to get advice from those with experience on what to do and what not to do. Jillian conducted a series of surveys and interviews with a cross-section of people and professionals in the field to compile this information, as well as collect best practices, tips and perspectives from divorced women with good intelligence to share. Jillian is now the CEO of a financial services marketing agency based in Toronto and New York and is happily remarried with two children.

She is also interested in receiving your feedback and stories at info@mydivorceguide.com.

Manufactured by Amazon.ca
Bolton, ON